DATE DUE

3/11/96			

Free Speech

From Newspapers to Music Lyrics

Free Speech

From Newspapers to Music Lyrics

Karen Zeinert

—Issues in Focus—

ENSLOW PUBLISHERS, INC.

44 Fadem Road	P.O. Box 38
Box 699	Aldershot
Springfield, N.J. 07081	Hants GU12 6BP
U.S.A.	U.K.

Library of Congress Cataloging-in-Publication Data

Zeinert, Karen.
      Free speech: from newspapers to music lyrics / Karen Zeinert.
         p. cm.—(Issues in focus)
      Includes bibliographical references (p.) and index.
      ISBN 0-89490-634-8
      1. Censorship—United States—Juvenile literature. 2. Freedom of the
press—United States—Juvenile literature. 3. Freedom of speech—United
States—Juvenile literature. [1. Freedom of speech. 2. Freedom of the press.
3. Censorship.] I. Title. II. Series: Issues in focus (Springfield, N.J.)
Z658.U5Z45   1995
323.44'5—dc20   94-34620
                                                         CIP
                                                         AC

Printed in the United States of America

10 9 8 7 6 5 4 3 2

Illustration Credits: ACLU, p. 33; Broadcast Pioneers Library, pp. 74, 80; *Des Moines Register*, p. 84; Educational Research Analysts, p. 37; Fuzzy Elsinger-Summers, p. 57; Eugene V. Debs Foundation, p. 93; Library of Congress, pp. 19, 24, 44, 66, 104, 107; Museum of the City of New York, p. 112; National Archives, pp. 89, 95; *St. Louis Post-Dispatch*, p. 14; Watchtower Bible and Tract Society of New York, Inc., p. 115; John Zeinert, pp. 9, 29, 42.

Cover Illustration: John A. Zeinert

Contents

1

The Debate About Free Speech

Shortly before classes were supposed to start in a middle school on the west side of Manhattan, a ten-year-old boy distributed pamphlets to fellow classmates. This pamphlet, which the boy had written, listed several reasons why he thought his principal should be fired. Needless to say, the publication caused quite a stir.

It didn't take long for the principal to notice the growing crowd of laughing children with some papers in their hands, and he thought it best to check out the situation immediately. A few minutes later, clutching one of the pamphlets in his fist, he stood in front of the young publisher. Without saying a word, he grabbed the remaining pamphlets from the boy's hands.

The boy insisted that his constitutional rights were being violated. The First Amendment to the Constitution, he said, gave him the right to publish his ideas, and no one, including the principal, had the right to seize his publication. The principal didn't agree, and he refused to return the boy's pamphlets.[1] Clearly, the First Amendment to the Constitution, which states several principles, including "Congress shall make no law . . . abridging [limiting] the freedom of speech . . . or the press," didn't mean the same thing to the boy as it did to his principal.

Their disagreement was not unusual. At times, the justices of the United States Supreme Court have failed to agree on what can be published or even what constitutes "speech" and should therefore be protected. Movies, for instance, were not considered worthy of First Amendment protection for many years nor were certain political ideas.

In general, every medium through which ideas can be expressed today, for example, newspapers, books, pictures, magazines, songs, radio and television broadcasts, movies, speeches, and demonstrations, is protected by the First Amendment. Even "silent speech," such as wearing armbands or burning the U.S. flag, is protected by the First Amendment because these actions can also express ideas. However, while these media are protected in general, this doesn't mean that specific books or songs or pamphlets about principals can't be banned. There are limits on speech.

What these limits should be has caused heated debates. Some Americans believe that free speech means that citizens should be able to read whatever they wish, publish anything they desire, listen to whomever they want, or see any movie they might like. They believe

Speech protected by the U.S. Constitution includes all forms of expression including, books, compact discs, magazines, television programs, movies, tapes, even campaign buttons. As a result, every American is affected by court rulings regarding this precious right.

they have the right to study all ideas so that they may pick the very best of the lot.

Others insist that words can shock and hurt, so there should be limits on what people, especially children and young adults, can read or hear or see. These people argue that the First Amendment was never intended to protect every word or idea an American states or prints. They would outlaw stories with four-letter words or magazines with pictures of naked men and women. In addition, they would limit what entertainers can sing on stage or say in films. The pamphlet the ten-year-old boy wrote embarrassed his principal and may have hurt his reputation. People who wish to limit speech might question whether or not the boy had the right to do this—his principal certainly did.

Because Americans haven't been able to agree on exactly what the First Amendment means, they have fought over the issue since the amendment was written. They have done so because they recognize the incredible power of words. When arguments can not be settled between two parties, the disputes are taken to court. A surprising number of cases, some of which are included in this book, were started on behalf of young people.

The courts' decisions establish the rules for America's media, some of which might reach millions of listeners or, as in the case of the ten-year-old boy, only a few readers. But even though we have many court decisions to serve as guidelines, this doesn't mean that the conflict about what can be said, read, or heard is finished. As you will see, the debate about free speech is far from settled, even if it has been going on for 200 years.

2

All the News
That's Fit to Print

On January 14, 1988, some high school students wore black armbands—a symbol of mourning—to their classes. They were very upset over a United States Supreme Court decision announced the day before that affected school newspapers. The Supreme Court's decision gave teachers and principals the right to censor, or cut, articles from school papers about controversial subjects, such as AIDS and abortion. These students were not about to accept censorship quietly, and in addition to wearing armbands, they argued about the case with their teachers.

The Supreme Court's decision also brought some strong protests from professional writers. Under headlines such as "Teacher Knows Best," journalists questioned the wisdom of the Supreme Court's action. An editor at *The Nation* magazine said, "The Court seems to hold that . . . debate on important issues should be kept from the school."[1] How, this writer wondered, would that enable students to become well-educated citizens? Others just wondered how such a thing could happen.

The 1988 decision grew out of an argument over what could and could not be printed in a newspaper at East Hazelwood High School, a school located in a suburb of St. Louis, Missouri. In late May 1983, the school's newspaper staff was busy checking the paper's proof pages (the first typeset copies) of the latest edition. This issue included articles about teenage pregnancy and the effects of divorce on children. These articles had been based on lengthy interviews with Hazelwood students.

The school's principal, Robert Reynolds, found out about the articles. After he read the proofs of the stories, he was very upset. He believed that readers would be able to identify the students interviewed, even though their names had been omitted to protect their privacy. In his opinion, this was a potentially embarrassing situation for these teenagers. The principal also objected to some of the information in the articles. There was no time to rewrite and reset the material and still be able to distribute the papers before the end of the school year, so Reynolds ordered the staff to drop the pages on which the controversial stories appeared.

Reynolds' action shocked the paper's staff and its editor, Cathy Kuhlmeier. They believed that their sources were not identifiable and that the articles were of great importance and interest. Furthermore, the staff refused to accept the idea that the principal had the right to force them to remove anything from their paper. That's censorship, they shouted. Weren't they protected by the First Amendment? Kuhlmeier decided to find the answer to this question by going to court.

After a five-year battle in lower courts, the case known as *Hazelwood School District* v. *Kuhlmeier* reached the United States Supreme Court. And here, in a 5 to 3 decision, the Court told Kuhlmeier that principals could indeed censor newspapers sponsored and funded by the school. The justices said that educators were to take into account the emotional maturity of the intended audience. If a newspaper advisor or principal thought the material was too upsetting for students to read, the educators had a right to cut it.

Justice Brennan didn't agree with the majority. In a strongly worded dissent he said that the majority had "violated the First Amendment's prohibitions against censorship of any student expression that neither disrupts classwork nor invades the rights of others." Brennan continued by pointing out that limiting expression could limit the students' education and "strangle the free mind."[2]

First Attempts to Censor Newspapers

The decision in the *Hazelwood* case wasn't the first argument about freedom of the press. The struggle over what can be said goes all the way back to the first newspapers, which were started in Europe in the 1500s.

Before printing presses were available, newspapers were written by hand and sold to subscribers. These papers contained military information, political gossip, jokes, scandals, and anything that would keep readers

Cathy Kuhlmeier, editor of the *Spectrum*, challenged her principal's right to censor the school's paper.

interested. Few people could read and write then or afford to buy the papers. Even so, many knew about them or heard about their contents by word of mouth.

Europe's rulers, mostly kings and queens, eventually learned that the papers criticized them, and they feared negative comments. They believed such remarks would cause their subjects to become disrespectful and difficult to rule. As a result, they tried to limit criticism by making it a crime to say anything negative about monarchs.

But because the papers were often written and distributed in secret, it was difficult for rulers to censor them. Nevertheless, they still tried to eliminate bad publicity. They severely punished the few publishers they managed to catch. The publishers were whipped, imprisoned, and even maimed, losing an ear or a hand for angering royalty. Yet, despite these horrible punishments, rulers were not able to control journalists.

England's Efforts to Control the Press

The situation became even more critical for royalty—especially in England—when printing presses became readily available in the 1600s. Presses could produce copies faster than handwriting, and publishers were able to reach thousands of people.

English rulers then tried to control the press by requiring anyone who wanted to publish a paper to have a royal license. This license gave rulers the right to review material before it was distributed. In addition, all printed material was supposed to carry a mark indicating that it had royal approval, and any reader possessing an unlicensed newspaper could be punished.

By the mid-1600s, England's king and Parliament,

which wanted more power, were nearing a showdown. A revolution took place in 1660 in which King Charles I literally lost his head and, for a short while, the monarchy was replaced with a new form of government.

During this time, Parliament became very strong and, even after the monarchy was restored, Parliament refused to give up its newly gained power. It gradually granted greater freedom to the press, which used this freedom to criticize the king and even Parliament, referring to one member as a "bald-headed buzzard." The practice of speaking one's mind spread from England to the British colonies in America.

Royal Governor Censors a Colonial Press

The first newspaper in the colonies was published on September 25, 1690. *Publick Occurrences, Both Forreign and Domestick* was written by Benjamin Harris in Boston, Massachusetts. Harris promised to expose rumors and print the names of all liars, which would have been a real threat to any leader.

The royal governor of the Massachusetts colony, Sir Edmund Andros, followed the old English tradition of licensing the press. He was under great pressure to censor any unflattering reports about the king or himself, for failure to do so could cost him his job.

So when Andros heard about *Publick Occurrences,* he was understandably concerned, especially since the publisher hadn't bothered to get a printing permit. After reading a copy of *Occurrences,* which contained an article attacking royalty, Andros ordered Harris to find and destroy all copies that had been distributed. The publisher agreed to do this, and his newspaper career ended after one issue.

Colonial Publisher Sets a Precedent for the Press

Other royal governors also tried to control the press. However, publishers began to defy the licensing laws, and by 1720, these laws were abandoned.

The governor of the New York colony, William Cosby, then turned to the courts to try to control printers who refused to publish only what the governor thought should appear in newspapers. He began his crusade with John Peter Zenger—a daring, defiant publisher who refused to be intimidated by any royal governor.

Zenger was one of the most popular printers in his colony. He was born in Germany in 1697, and he immigrated to New York City with his family when he was thirteen years old. Like many boys of his day, he was apprenticed to an employer. He agreed to work for a printer for eight years in exchange for being taught a trade. After leaving the printer's office, Zenger eventually set up his own press.

In 1733, Zenger decided to start a newspaper, and the first issue of his New York *Weekly Journal* appeared on November 5. At this time, there was great controversy surrounding Cosby. Even though he had only been in charge of the colony for one year, Cosby was accused of many wrongdoings, and Zenger told readers all about them in the *Journal.* His paper was popular from the start.

An embarrassed Cosby began his campaign to shut

down the *Journal*—and make an example of Zenger—shortly after the first issue appeared. Cosby ordered the colony's chief justice, James De Lancey, to get a grand jury to charge the publisher with printing seditious libel, that is, *any* statement, true or false, that would encourage disrespect for royalty, a crime under English law.

De Lancey followed Cosby's orders. He assembled a grand jury, but despite his emotional pleas, the jury refused to charge Zenger with a crime. Cosby was furious.

Although Zenger knew he was in great danger, he continued his attacks, and an enraged Cosby had the printer arrested on November 17, 1734. After several questionable legal maneuvers on the part of the governor, Zenger was brought to trial on August 4, 1735.

Zenger's supporters found one of the best lawyers in the colonies, Andrew Hamilton, to defend their friend. Hamilton was as brave as he was skilled, and he refused to accept the old seditious libel law. He ignored the chief justice's arguments that a critical statement about a leader was enough to send a man to prison.

Instead, Hamilton made an appeal to the jury. In a courtroom filled with spectators, he told the jury that it should not punish a man because he criticized his ruler—governor or king—*if the man told the truth.* "The words," Hamilton said, "must be false, scandalous and seditious, or else we are not guilty."[3]

The jury accepted Hamilton's argument, and it set Zenger free. In doing so, the jury established a precedent that is certainly followed today—American newspapers can criticize the government. It is hoped that by publishing the good and bad deeds that leaders do, voters will be able to make wise choices when they elect their leaders.

Andrew Hamilton defended John Peter Zenger, a newspaper editor, in a dramatic trial about free speech held on August 4, 1735.

Colonial Newspapers Wield Great Power

The press immediately put its newfound freedom to use. In the 1760s, for example, shortly after King George III began his rule in England, the press made many attacks on the king's policies. When one of the king's ministers proposed a stamp tax, a tax on all printed goods, the papers lost no time in denouncing the money-raising scheme. Most newspaper publishers barely made a profit, and the tax would have driven some of them out of business.

The press was joined by colonial leaders who were deeply concerned about how the tax came about. Parliament had passed the law without consulting the colonies, and colonial leaders thought that was unfair. They wrote editorials for local papers that turned many colonists against the king and his governors, and soon "No taxation without representation!" was being shouted everywhere. The colonies were so swept up in a spirit of revolt that Parliament was forced to drop the tax.

The colonial press was delighted with the part it played in getting the British to back down. Twenty-three papers, most with a circulation of two thousand or less, had wielded great power.

Colonial papers then turned their attention to the whole matter of how the king and the English Parliament governed the colonies. The papers hammered away at the rulers' mistakes, and many historians believe the press had a great influence in rousing the colonists to revolt.

After the Revolutionary War ended, leaders in the colonies were very careful to protect the freedoms for which the colonists had fought. They drafted the Bill of Rights, ten amendments to the Constitution, which, among other things, guaranteed Americans the precious right of freedom of speech. The Bill of Rights went into effect in 1791.

American Newspapers Expand

Americans were hungry for news, and over the next two hundred years, the number of newspapers being printed increased dramatically. By 1890, more than eight million copies were distributed daily, and there were close to one thousand different papers from which to choose. By 1990, more than seventy million papers were printed daily.

Competition for readers among publishers was keen, and editors were under great pressure to find interesting stories to get readers to buy their papers. Besides acting as a watchdog over the government, papers ran articles on topics such as sports, business, and important people of the day—especially if they were involved in a shocking scandal. This raised the question of the invasion of privacy, but when editors were challenged in court, newspapers were usually given the right to print whatever they believed was newsworthy. If the papers printed lies, though, anyone hurt by the falsehoods could sue the papers.

Newspapers During Wartime

The major exceptions to complete freedom of the press—aside from printing falsehoods—happened during wartime. In 1918, for instance, Congress passed the Sedition Act. This act made it illegal to criticize the government. Most Americans supported the act because the United States was involved in World War I, and they believed it was important for the country to be united during such a trying time. This law was repealed in 1921, three years after the war ended.

During America's participation in World War II (1941–1945), the press censored itself. It was careful to avoid giving out any information that might be of use to America's enemies, Japan, Germany, and Italy, or giving the impression that the country was anything but united and determined to win the war.

The press's position in the Vietnam conflict (1954–1973) differed from the one held throughout World Wars I and II. Unlike previous wars, the Vietnam conflict divided America, and some newspapers openly criticized the government from the beginning of the war. When American participation, which began with some military aid, escalated into a full-scale war that appeared to have no end in sight, many Americans began to question their government's decision to continue to fight. Although government leaders fumed and fussed at antiwar newspapers, which they sometimes blamed for the number of Americans turning against the war, leaders, at first, made no attempt to censor papers.

But the government's position on censorship changed in 1971. It was then that Daniel Ellsberg, a consultant for a private research firm, discovered a top secret government report that contained information about how the war had been conducted as well as sensitive information about secret negotiations the government had held with other countries. Ellsberg thought the public should know the report's contents.

When he gave part of the report to the *New York Times*, which printed several sections, the government was horrified at the thought of its secrets being made public, and it went to court to stop publication.

This case was rushed to the U.S. Supreme Court, where arguments were heard only seventeen days after the first part of the report appeared in the *Times*. The government argued that printing the papers would hurt national security. Ellsberg and the newspaper's editor said that the papers contained information that the public needed to know, and they added, they had the right to print the material. They pointed out that "prior restraint," the need for a publisher to have permission to print from government officials, had been struck down long ago.

The Supreme Court agreed with Ellsberg and the *Times* in a 6 to 3 decision, making it very difficult for the government to stop any paper from publishing what it wanted to publish, even in wartime. Justice Hugo Black said that the press had a responsibility to "bare the secrets of government and inform the people." He added, "Only a free and unrestrained press can effectively expose deception in government. And paramount among the responsibilities of a free press is the duty to prevent any part of the government from deceiving the people and sending them off to distant lands to die of foreign fevers and foreign shot and shell."[4]

Perhaps that is why many people felt that the *Hazelwood* decision was a step backwards in time. Since the first student publications in 1777, students had gained greater freedom over the years to publish information editors believed readers needed to know, just as professional

The U.S. Supreme Court consists of nine justices who are appointed for life. Shown here is the Supreme Court of 1972, (front row, left to right) Justices Potter Stewart, William O. Douglas, Warren E. Burger (Chief Justice at the time), William J. Brennan, Byron R. White, (back row) Lewis F. Powell, Thurgood Marshall, Harry A. Blackmun, and William Rehnquist, now the Chief Justice.

newspapers had. In 1988, that trend ended because the Supreme Court wanted to protect young people from disturbing information. And it wasn't alone. Many school boards and parents had fought over information in various textbooks for years, verbal fights that sometimes turned violent.

3

Get Rid of That Book!

In the fall of 1974, more than eight thousand students refused to attend classes in Kanawha County, West Virginia. Parents formed picket lines around the county's schools to prevent children who might want to enter from doing so, and a local minister asked parents to pray that three county school board members would die. Meanwhile, demonstrators fired at several school buses when drivers began their routes. It was a bitter, angry demonstration, to say the least.

This demonstration grew out of an argument over English textbooks that the school system had purchased during the summer. Many parents considered these books unfit for classroom use, as did one of the school board members, who said the books were "disrespectful

of authority and religion . . . obscene, [and] unpatriotic."[1]

Three of the school board's five members and the
county's teachers didn't agree with the protesters, and
teachers used the texts in class. Protesters reacted by trying to shut down the schools so the children couldn't
read the books, and when that tactic failed, by having
three board members and the county's superintendent
arrested for contributing to the delinquency of minors. It
would take months to work out a compromise on the
texts, years to heal the communities torn apart by the
printed word.

Early Attempts to Censor Books

Protesters in Kanawha County were following an old tradition when they tried to control what others read. More
than two thousand years ago, kings tried to get rid of
books that challenged their right to rule. Religious leaders, who were very powerful then, thought that books
that promoted different faiths or different moral standards were dangerous as well, and they used their power
to eliminate these texts. Both kings and religious leaders
took steps to make sure that certain books were destroyed.

Although early royal and religious censors were able
to destroy many books of which they didn't approve,
rulers from the 1500s on had great difficulty doing so.
Printing presses were common by then, and they could
produce thousands of copies quickly. Rulers then posted
lists of forbidden books, and monarchs punished booksellers who sold the banned books as well as publishers

Sometimes Americans have burned books they think are obscene or offensive in order to draw attention to their cause—getting rid of such books in their communities.

who printed them. Even so, forbidden books did not disappear.

Attempts at Book Censorship in Colonial America

English leaders also tried to limit what books colonial Americans could read, but they were no more successful in this endeavor than they were in controlling what colonists read in newspapers. In general, the colonists were a feisty group, and they did not like taking orders from royalty, especially when it came to what they should think or what they could read.

The First Amendment Protects Books

The demand to read whatever one wished was as strong as ever after the Revolutionary War. The men who wrote the Constitution forbade Congress to pass any laws that would censor the press, and they denied religious leaders any political power. As a result, although political and religious leaders could suggest that Americans ignore certain books, these leaders could not ban any text.

However, it was generally agreed that the Constitution did not protect every book. No writer could publish a book of lies about his neighbors, for example, and expect the First Amendment to protect him. The First Amendment also did not protect obscenity, which was believed to undermine Americans' morals, or books that might endanger national security. The difficulty that arose was determining what was libelous, obscene, or dangerous. This task was left up to the courts.

First Attempts to Ban Books

Unlike journalists, who were limited to reporting real events, novelists—in theory—were free to write about any topic they might wish. However, if the story included any four-letter words or mentioned sex, authors were well aware that they might be accused of writing obscene literature. Although many authors censored themselves to avoid trouble, a few chose to write about life as they saw it. These writers often had difficulty finding a publisher who would print their works. Still, some controversial books made their way into bookstores.

Even though some citizens had complained about books they considered obscene for many years, the first case wasn't brought to court until 1821. At that time, the chief judge of the Massachusetts Supreme Court, Isaac Parker, heard arguments against a book titled *Memoirs of a Woman of Pleasure*, which had been written by John Cleland. This book, a biography of a prostitute, had been published in England under the title *Fanny Hill*. The book's controversial contents caused such an uproar in England that the book was outlawed there. An American publisher, Peter Holmes, eventually obtained printing rights and, shortly after, the book appeared in some bookstores in America, including a few shops in Massachusetts. Some outraged citizens in the state wanted the book banned, and they turned to Judge Parker for help. After merely hearing about the contents of *Memoirs of a Woman of Pleasure*, he decided that the book was "lewd, wicked, scandalous, infamous, and obscene."[2] The biography, Parker said, was to be banned in the state. The out-of-state publisher was beyond the

31

reach of Massachusetts authorities, but local booksellers weren't, and they were to be punished if they carried *Memoirs of a Woman of Pleasure*.

Encouraged by such a decision, would-be censors in other states decided to ban certain books too. By the mid-1800s, a crusade for high morals was in full swing.

One of the best known crusaders of the day was Anthony Comstock. He followed very strict standards, and he expected everyone else to live by the same rules. Comstock was especially appalled by literature he considered obscene, and he set out to rid the whole country of such books, a task to which he devoted forty years of his life.

Although a law banning obscene materials from the mail had been passed in 1865, officials could do little unless the person who ordered the material complained to postal authorities, and this was not likely to happen. Comstock saw the mail as the main source of material he deemed disgusting, and he believed that if he could shut down this source, he could put an end to "filthy" books. In 1872, he began a successful campaign for a national law that allowed postal inspectors to check the mail's contents, remove obscene literature, and arrest publishers.

Comstock was then appointed as one of the inspectors, and he found lots of objectionable books. When he retired, he claimed he "had convicted persons enough to fill a passenger train of 61 coaches . . . and destroyed 160 tons of obscene literature."[3]

Although most people appeared to favor censorship in the late 1800s, standards began to change in the 1900s. Members of Clean Books Leagues and censors were ridiculed. Judges were less willing to declare something

Roger Baldwin founded the American Civil Liberties Union (ACLU) in 1920. He had become very angry at the numerous attempts of the government to limit constitutional rights, and he decided to start an organization that would defend these liberties.

obscene, and some publishers openly challenged a state's right to censor, claiming, under the Fourteenth Amendment, that states could not deny any citizens rights that were guaranteed under the First Amendment, and that included freedom of the press. As a result, books of all kinds were readily available.

Clashes Over Textbooks

Nevertheless, the attempts of citizens to choose the books others could read did not stop. This was especially true in the classroom. Here, unlike a public or school library where readers could avoid books that might offend them, all children—it was believed—would read their textbooks. And not all parents liked the texts' contents. Some feared that certain stories or ideas might undermine their children's religious beliefs or moral standards, and they wanted the objectionable materials banned from the classroom.

Some parents and concerned citizens had questioned books used in classrooms for many years. Before the Civil War (1861–1865), for example, Southerners objected to social studies books, most of which were printed in the North, that favored the North or spoke poorly of slavery. To avoid losing sales, some textbook publishers printed two versions, one for the North and another for the South, a practice that continued for more than one hundred years.

In the 1920s, science books came under fire. Biology texts that included Darwin's theory of evolution, which stated that man and apes had descended over millions of years from a common ancestor, shocked devoutly religious parents. They believed the Bible's explanation that man was created directly by God, and they did not want children exposed to what they considered to be anti-religious views. And they were not alone. So many citizens wanted the biblical version taught that some state legislatures were pressured into passing laws stating that teachers could not discuss evolution in the classroom.

To please as many parents as possible, textbook companies included the biblical explanation as well as Darwin's theory. This didn't satisfy parents who wanted to eliminate any mention of evolution, then or now. Today, wherever religious groups that interpret the Bible literally are very strong, the struggle continues over whether or not the theory of evolution should be included in texts.

English texts and reading books also came under fire over the years. As various groups struggled for respect and equality, they challenged some books being assigned as classroom reading. One of the assignments that received the most attacks was Shakespeare's *The Merchant of Venice*. Critics believed the play portrayed Jews as mean, greedy people and encouraged Americans to hate them. Others attacked Mark Twain's *Huckleberry Finn* because it used the objectionable word "nigger." Women were upset because they were seldom portrayed as leaders, and Native Americans and Latinos were upset because they weren't mentioned at all.

In the 1950s, social studies texts were once again under scrutiny. Communism appeared to be thriving in what was then known as the Soviet Union, and when the Soviets threatened to take over the world, many Americans genuinely thought they were in danger. Some Americans also believed that communists were at work in this country, undermining democracy every way they could. This included, they believed, putting passages in textbooks that made the Soviet system appeal to young people. Textbook companies had to prove that their authors were not communists or lose sales.

Years of Change and Challenge

Conflicts over what could be read in class didn't end in the 1950s. In fact, by the early 1970s, there was widespread concern over materials used in schools, and parents as well as concerned citizens insisted on having a greater voice in what was being taught.

This demand was caused, in part, by the tremendous changes that occurred in American society in the 1960s. For example, civil rights legislation ended a one-hundred-year-old policy of racial segregation in public schools. At the same time, Americans were deeply divided over the war in Vietnam, and many young men refused to register for military service, an act many older people considered unpatriotic and offensive. In addition, women were demanding equal rights, and teenagers were more sexually active than ever before.

Some Americans looked about for someone or something to blame for the changes they considered harmful, and they chose the schools for their scapegoat. The classroom, these people said, was full of un-American, immoral ideas, many of which came from textbooks. These people were conservative in their views, that is they wanted old beliefs and customs upheld and rules strictly enforced.

At the same time, other citizens looked about themselves and welcomed change, especially the progress

Mel and Norma Gabler became deeply upset about the contents of their children's textbooks in the 1960s. As a result, they decided to start Educational Research Analysts in Longview, Texas, an organization that would alert textbook committees to material that offended conservative standards.

made on equal rights for African Americans, women, and minority groups. They pleaded for more toleration of differences, and they shunned strict discipline. These people were called liberals.

Because so much had changed, educators believed that current lessons and textbooks no longer met the needs of children, and many school systems—after heated debates in teachers' meetings—tossed out the old curriculum, made new lesson plans, and started to look for new textbooks. They also looked for authors who spoke for minorities so that all Americans would be represented. Needless to say, a clash between conservative and liberal parents, both equally devoted to the idea of providing the best possible education for children, was unavoidable.

Not all clashes produced bitter protests like the demonstration in Kanawha County. However, many parents have become upset enough to go to court to try to have texts or library books removed from local schools. In most cases, judges have refused to allow committees to ban schoolbooks in classrooms or books in school libraries unless the books were out-of-date (especially true of science books) or inappropriately chosen. Content, vocabulary, and the age of the readers are taken into account. A story about a teenager who takes his own life, for example, would probably not be acceptable reading for first graders but might be considered appropriate reading for high school seniors.

A U.S. District Court judge in Massachusetts, Joseph Tauro, summed up the position held by many courts today when he announced his decision in the *Right to Read Defense Committee of Chelsea* v. *School Committee of the*

City of Chelsea case on July 5, 1978. After listening to many arguments about banning controversial books in Chelsea's schools, Tauro said that "a school should be a readily accessible warehouse of ideas."[4] Committees could add as many books as they wished in order to present many views and beliefs. However, they could not take away even a single page just because it offended them. Even so, some committees, liberal and conservative, still try to have only one side—their side—presented in the classroom.

4

Magazines and Morals

Although some articles in young people's magazines such as *Sassy* may raise a few eyebrows, few articles that appear in approximately one hundred juvenile periodicals each month shock or offend. Editors of children's publications want to publish the best magazine possible, and this includes refusing to print stories that might embarrass or shock readers.

To accomplish their goals, editors spell out what they are looking for in their guidelines for writers. Writers must follow these guidelines if they wish to sell their work. Although requirements vary from publisher to publisher, many guides list acceptable topics for nonfiction and suggested story ideas for fiction. Some religious magazines even list acceptable appearance and behavior for fictional characters. Girls, for example, may not wear slacks or makeup, and heroes and heroines may not be

Children have more than one hundred magazines from which to choose.

disrespectful to their elders or swear or smoke or take drugs.

Few children's writers complain about these restrictions. Like editors, they want to protect readers from sexually explicit material and violent characters. Sometimes, however, certain groups in society would like to protect everyone from what they consider shocking, immoral material in magazines.

Early American Magazines

The first American magazines were printed in the 1700s. Competitors Ben Franklin and John Webbe published *General Magazine* and *The American Magazine* only a few days apart in 1741. Their publications, like those that quickly followed, were similar to English magazines. They were primarily written for well-educated readers.

In the 1800s, a variety of magazines began to appear. Most, like *North American Review, Harper's,* and *The Atlantic Monthly*, still appealed to intellectuals, though. Even so, interest ran high since magazines offered information not found in newspapers or books, and by the mid-1800s, there were more than six hundred publications from which to choose.

Growing Interest in Magazines

By the early 1900s, several thousand publications were available. Unlike America's early magazines, most of these publications, for example, *The Saturday Evening Post*, were designed to appeal to average citizens. Many magazines were readily available. Most sold for ten cents, and they could be obtained through a subscription or purchased at local newsstands.

This 1900 newsstand is not all that different from modern newsstands located on street corners today. In fact, some of the popular magazines published then are still being published.

At the same time, a new kind of publication appeared, the "girlie" magazine. These publications, which usually featured pictures of young women wearing very few clothes, caused quite an uproar. As more and more shocking pictures appeared, cries for censorship could be heard all over the country. Most censorship attempts were led by religious organizations and women's groups who were concerned about morals in America. These censors were also afraid that girlie magazines might be seen by children.

Legislative Attempt to Censor Magazines

In 1927, legislation was introduced in Congress to control the content of magazines. But despite emotional pleas from the representatives who wanted to establish a national board for magazine censorship, Congress refused to pass the bill. Opponents argued that the First Amendment prohibited them from establishing any bureau designed to limit freedom of the press.

Citizens Use Pressure to Ban Magazines

When legislation failed to abolish controversial magazines, some citizens took matters into their own hands. They used pressure to shut down local newsstands and bookstores that carried so-called immoral materials. Religious leaders encouraged followers to boycott (stop buying) all products from any outlet—newsstands, bookstores, and corner drugstores—that carried materials the leaders thought were obscene. Sometimes these censors picketed stores to encourage others not to enter them or to embarrass them if they did. These tactics were quite successful, especially in small towns.

Post Office Officials Try to Censor Magazines

From the mid-1800s, postal authorities had the right to confiscate obscene material mailed in the United States or sent to Americans from abroad. But this practice was challenged in 1933, when a postal inspector seized a copy of James Joyce's *Ulysses*, a book that had been ordered from Europe by an American publisher so that it might be copied and distributed in the United States. Although *Ulysses* was considered a controversial book even in Europe, the publisher thought the text had great merit. Willing to fight for the right to print *Ulysses*, the publisher went to court to get his book back.

The courts sided with the publisher. The first judge to hear the case, John M. Woolsey, found *Ulysses* a sincere and serious attempt to devise "a new literary method for the observation and description of mankind."[1] When the postal system appealed the case, the next judge praised *Ulysses* for its originality and refused to call it obscene just because it contained some four-letter words. These decisions seriously challenged the postal system's ability to recognize obscene material.

Even so, postal inspectors continued to put pressure on publishers of so-called obscene materials, and they seized magazines for many years. Surprisingly, few publishers challenged the inspectors' decisions, for when they did, they usually won.

For instance, in 1946, postal authorities decided to try to censor *Esquire*, then a controversial magazine for men. An inspector, after viewing the magazine's contents, proposed to take away *Esquire*'s second-class

46

mailing privilege, a move that would cost *Esquire* more than $500,000 in increased postage. The inspector argued that second-class privileges were supposed to be limited to publishers who made a real contribution to the public welfare, and he didn't see anything on the pages of *Esquire* that even came close to contributing something of value to anyone.

Since paying first-class mailing fees would have forced *Esquire* to raise its selling price and it might lose subscribers as a result, the publisher decided to fight the inspector's decision all the way to the Supreme Court. When the justices heard this case, they didn't attempt to decide whether or not *Esquire* made a significant contribution. Rather, they looked at the dangers of censorship. The justices believed that if they allowed this postal official to punish *Esquire* because he didn't approve of the magazine, other magazines might also be censored in the same way. The Supreme Court said, "To withdraw the second-class rate from this publication today because its contents seemed to one official not good for the public would sanction withdrawals of the second-class rate tomorrow from another periodical whose social or economic views seemed harmful to another official."[2] As a result, *Esquire*, much to the disgust of the postal inspector, was given back its second-class mailing privilege.

Even though the post office lost the *Esquire* case, inspectors still continued to seize materials. But the courts usually refused to label the magazines in question obscene, no matter how awful they appeared to be in postal officials' opinions.

Censors Lose More Ground in the 1950s

Censors became distraught over Supreme Court decisions in the 1950s. Not only did the Supreme Court see little that it considered obscene, it struck down some state antiobscenity laws, claiming they violated the First Amendment. Although the Supreme Court did find a bookseller, Samuel Roth, guilty of selling obscene material in 1957, many cases censors fought hard to win were lost.

Each case centered on the definition of obscenity, which varied from judge to judge and community to community. Rather than take the side of the censors, the Supreme Court appeared to narrow its definition of obscenity with every case. As a result, by 1960, nothing could be banned unless the Supreme Court was absolutely convinced that the material in question, which had to be judged as a whole, was so bad, so lewd, so vulgar, it was "utterly without redeeming social importance."[3] This meant that a magazine probably couldn't be banned if it had one idea worth reading, and this enraged censors.

A Victory for Censors

But just when those who wanted to ban certain materials were about to give up, the Supreme Court, on March 21, 1966, upheld a lower court's verdict against magazine publisher, Ralph Ginzburg. Ginzburg published *Eros* magazine, which he sold through the mail. Critics were outraged by the magazine's content, which they thought was nothing more than smut.

The courts were more upset over Ginzburg's actions than they were about his magazine. Several justices believed

48

Ginzburg was not even trying to present anything of value to the public. Instead, he was using every available means to appeal to prurient (indecent) interests to make money. Justice Brennan was especially appalled by ads and promotions that promised future articles titled "Was Shakespeare a Homosexual?" and "Sex in the Supermarket."[4] Although such titles probably wouldn't shock readers today, they disgusted most citizens thirty years ago. Because the justices couldn't find one shred of value in Ginzburg's publications, his conviction was upheld in a 5 to 4 decision. A flabbergasted Ginzburg, who believed his work was protected by the First Amendment, was ordered to pay fines totaling $28,000 and was whisked off to jail for a five-year sentence.

But in spite of the results of the Ginzburg case, censorship of material, even magazines most people would call hard-core pornography, became very difficult from 1970 on. Although the Supreme Court gave communities more power to regulate obscene material in the *Miller* v. *California* decision in 1973, many communities chose not to try to define obscenity or to try to limit what local citizens could read.

A New Censorship Tactic Is Tried

As publishers became more and more daring in the 1980s, and pornographic magazines regularly pictured women being humiliated, beaten, or raped, some women's groups decided to try to shut down questionable publications by using a new approach. Led by Catharine MacKinnon, a professor of law at the University of Michigan, women's groups decided not to argue whether or not these publications were obscene. Instead,

49

for the first time, they claimed that such publications violated women's civil rights. MacKinnon and her supporters argued that magazines that pictured women as victims encouraged readers to think about women as second-class citizens, threatening their economic opportunities, their quality of life, and even their lives.

At least eight city councils across the nation accepted the women's arguments: Minneapolis, Minnesota; Detroit, Michigan; Des Moines, Iowa; Omaha, Nebraska; Columbus and Cincinnati, Ohio; St. Louis, Missouri; and Madison, Wisconsin. These councils passed resolutions that made it possible for their cities to ban material women found demeaning and threatening.

Critics of censorship fought hard to stop the resolutions. They argued that although many studies have been conducted about pornography and its effects, few studies have shown that men who read obscene material are more demeaning or violent toward women than men who don't read the magazines. Also, they voiced concern over a new tactic to try to censor the press. Almost any group, the critics argued, could claim a publication pictured them in unflattering terms, encouraging the courts to ban anything that might be controversial. The best way to deal with upsetting publications, the critics continued, was to publish material that presented the other side. The courts agreed. Wherever the new resolutions were challenged, they were struck down because they violated the First Amendment.

Today, Americans have an estimated twenty-two thousand different magazines from which to choose. They include news magazines such as *Time*, the latest information about television programs, *TV Guide*®, and thousands of highly specialized journals, including *Underwater Technology* and *California Horse Review.* Not all newsstands could possibly carry every magazine available, but most try to display as many different titles as possible, so all readers can find something that is of interest to them. Stores that carry magazines that some citizens would call obscene usually restrict entry to only adults to protect children—a compromise that appears to be working, although it doesn't please everyone.

5

Music to My Ears

On December 29, 1992, Ice-T, a rapper turned hard-rocker, and his band, Body Count, appeared in Green Bay, Wisconsin. In the auditorium, more than one thousand fans cheered loudly when Ice-T announced he would be doing "Cop Killer," a song that had raised so much controversy it had been withdrawn from one of Ice-T's albums.

Outside, one hundred policemen picketed the show, and several carried pictures of policemen who had been killed in the line of duty. Because a threat of a drive-by shooting had been called into police headquarters, protection was provided for the pickets. Once again, feelings ran high over what should not be said, even when the words are sung.

Ability of Music to Influence People

Music has long been thought of as a means of communication. For instance, at wedding dances, musicians often play polkas or other peppy music to show joy, and they select slow, somber tunes for funerals to express sorrow. Feelings of patriotism can be aroused by listening to marching music or singing one's national anthem.

Because music can influence people's feelings, some rulers have tried to control it. In China, for example, western symphonies were banned for many years because they were somehow considered a threat to national security. Why these leaders believed that hearing music from the West might somehow weaken their rule isn't clear. What is clear, though, is the fact that they haven't been alone. Even today, there is an ongoing discussion about censoring music, a practice that started in the colonies.

Colonial Governor Bans Songs

Governor Cosby, the colonial governor of New York who had such a difficult time trying to control what newspapers said about the king of England, was responsible for controlling what was sung in his colony. When song sheets Cosby considered disrespectful to the king appeared in New York, the governor tried to eliminate the lyrics and punish their writers. He insisted that all copies of the songs, which he called "scandalous," be rounded up and burned. Then he offered a reward of twenty pounds—no small sum in the 1700s—to anyone who would identify the authors of the song sheets. However, he was unable to find the men or women who wrote the lyrics.

Pleased by Cosby's reaction, colonists continued to

use songs to torment the English. During the Revolutionary War, for instance, colonial prisoners of war held in ships off the coast of New York City regularly angered their guards by singing patriotic songs. As soon as the guards went on deck to get some fresh air, the prisoners began to sing. Guards then either had to endure the stuffy, smelly, overcrowded ship's hold with their prisoners or suffer insults sung by hundreds of colonists.

No Threat of Censorship for Almost Two Hundred Years

After the war, little thought was given to controlling music until the 1950s. At that time, the American economy was growing rapidly. Children were given larger allowances than ever before, and because so many jobs were available, many teenagers took part-time positions. As a result, they had real buying power, and businesses were not unaware of this fact.

Record companies, eager for teenagers' business, began to market songs that especially would appeal to young people. To build a loyal following, recording stars traveled throughout the United States giving live performances. These entertainers chose several ways to make themselves different from singers who wanted to appeal to adults. One way to do this was to openly display emotion on stage. Teenage idol Johnny Ray actually cried when he sang about romances and broken hearts.

Another technique these performers used was to have a band that used a strong—really strong!—back beat, creating music that invited lively dancing. Teenagers across the country ignored waltzes and fox trots and learned steps they could use to jukebox hits like "Rock

Around the Clock," belted out by Bill Haley and the Comets.

But of all the entertainers who gained the attention of teenagers at the time, none was as well-received as Elvis Presley. Not only did he display emotion and have a band that could produce loud music with a strong beat, Presley went one step further. He provided action—swiveling hips and some fancy steps—that caused young girls to scream and even faint. His performance was so controversial at the time that television producers were hesitant to have him appear on their programs, even though Elvis would attract thousands of viewers. Producers finally decided to include Elvis's act, but only if they could tone down—censor—his presentation. As a result, Elvis was filmed only from the waist up.

Parents became alarmed at the new music with which they couldn't identify. They began to wonder if such music wasn't lowering their children's morals or at least affecting their hearing. Still, there was little attempt to control what records all children could hear or what entertainers they could see. Rather, if any limits were set, they were set on an individual basis in each home.

Changes in Music Over the Next Thirty Years

Lyrics, like books and magazines in the following years, became more daring. Besides singing songs about young love, entertainers began to include songs that questioned authority, used some four-letter words, and seemed to encourage violence. Many entertainers tried to increase their following by including controversial songs in their

This group, Dizzy Lane, sings controversial songs, a right protected by the First Amendment.

albums as well as performing questionable actions on and off the stage.

Demands for Censorship

Parents, especially conservative parents, and other concerned adults reacted to the changes in music by calling for censorship. To bolster their argument for limiting what songs could be sung, parents pointed to violent acts that occurred during and after concerts. They believed that the music was responsible for the violence.

One of the first outbreaks of violence took place in the summer of 1956. A film entitled "Rock Around the Clock," featuring Bill Haley, included lots of music. At the film's height, that is, when the music was the loudest and wildest, teenagers got up and danced in the theaters' aisles. Dancing soon turned to destruction, as movie-goers "ripped up seats, hit each other, and destroyed anything they could lay their hands on."[1] Supporters of rock and roll thought the actions were nothing more than natural teenage rebellion. Parents thought they were frightening. As incidents continued over the years, police and security guards were hired to prevent violence from erupting, rather than stop the performances.

The debate over whether or not an entertainer's words cause violence has continued for almost forty years. After a recent concert in Seattle, Washington, where rapper Ice Cube described police violence and gunplay, members of the audience began fighting among themselves, and five who carried guns to the concert fired at least sixty shots, hitting four people. Critics of rap blamed Ice Cube's performance.[2]

However, performers such as M. C. Ren insist that

entertainers' words, whether given in a live performance or recorded on a record or compact disc, are not responsible for violent outbreaks. After being questioned about his controversial records, Ren said, "A record can't make nobody do anything. Sometimes doing a record is just my way of getting back. . . . I can speak out. When people listen to the record, that's their way of speaking back. They put it in their car and bump it up as loud as they can."[3]

Cities Censor Songs

Like parents, city councils throughout the country were also concerned about the lyrics entertainers were singing on local stages and selling at the music stores. Relying on a 1973 Supreme Court decision (*Miller* v. *California*), which gave cities more control over regulating obscenity, many councils passed ordinances that outlawed "obscene" songs.

The first obscenity conviction occurred in 1990. Broward County officials in Florida declared that a song sung by 2 Live Crew, "As Nasty As They Wanna Be," was obscene. Local music stores pulled the record, and the leader of the group, Luther Campbell, was arrested after he sang "As Nasty As They Wanna Be" in a concert in Broward. A local court upheld Broward officials' actions. "As Nasty As They Wanna Be," the judge said, was indeed obscene.[4]

But censors' celebrations were short-lived. This case was highly publicized, and curious teens across the country bought the song in record numbers wherever it was available. Within a short time, it had sold almost two

59

million copies. Clearly, censors said, this was not the way to go.

Not only did the legal struggle over "As Nasty As They Wanna Be" create a lot of publicity and sales for 2 Live Crew, the struggle also ended in a legal victory for the group. An appeal was filed in a circuit court (*Luke Records, Inc.* v. *Navallo*), and in 1992, the court reversed the previous decision, giving 2 Live Crew the right to sing its song.

Labeling Songs

In 1985, five years before 2 Live Crew was arrested, Tipper Gore, wife of Al Gore, now the Vice President of the United States, and other concerned parents formed the Parents' Music Resource Center (PMRC). These parents listened to many popular albums and, alarmed by the lyrics they heard, asked for a hearing before the United States Senate. The PMRC wanted to draw national attention to songs the parents thought were harmful to children and to explore ways to keep these songs away from young people. Representatives from recording companies also testified before the Senate. They defended their clients and insisted on the right of freedom of speech.

Eventually, a compromise was worked out. From 1990 on, records—and now compact discs—that contained language that the PMRC thought might be inappropriate for children would carry labels reading "Parental Advisory, Explicit Lyrics." This way, no songs would be censored, but parents would be made aware of the fact that they might want to listen to some discs before allowing their children to hear them.

Questions About Music in Schools

While some parents were struggling with how best to deal with obscene lyrics at the record store, other parents were struggling with the question of religious music in schools, especially at Christmas. Many schools include carols, "Silent Night," for instance, in their Christmas concerts. But not all students who attend public schools are Christians, and some parents have complained loudly about including such music in public programs. Because the U.S. Constitution strictly forbids any public institution from favoring or encouraging any particular religion, some parents believe singing Christian songs is unconstitutional.

A few have taken the issue to court. In general, schools have been allowed to continue to use such music because, as a judge in South Dakota said, Christmas carols have become part of "our national culture and heritage."[5]

To avoid more court cases, school systems that want to continue to use religious music usually spell out their reasons for doing so very carefully so that parents understand why such music is being taught. The State Board of Education in California is a leader in this area. It developed guidelines that instruct all teachers who include religious music in class to make sure that students understand that these songs are being included as part of a study of the history of American music, a history that includes a wide variety of melodies and content. And there is such variety because, to date, censors have not been able to ban any song nationwide.

Movies, Censors, and Codes

For almost ninety years, Americans have argued about how children are affected by movies—especially those containing lots of violence. The National Institute of Mental Health claims that such films have increased fearfulness in children as well as made them less sensitive to human suffering. This institute also believes that violent movies tend to make children think that using brute force is an acceptable way to solve a problem.[1] Although not all Americans agree with the institute's position, and several other studies have not reached the same conclusions, many Americans believe that children should not be allowed to see every film that's shown today, which is hardly a new idea.

First Motion Pictures

The first motion picture theater opened in Los Angeles,

California, in 1902. Admission to see a one-hour silent film was ten cents. People packed this theater daily, and it wasn't long before other entrepreneurs decided to copy the idea. Soon theaters were opening all over America.

By 1907, there were also five thousand nickelodeons, theaters that charged a nickel for a twenty-minute film. Some nickelodeons were set up in shabby buildings near saloons. This, plus the fact that these places were often kept open all night and always kept dark, distressed local high-minded citizens. What, they wondered aloud, was happening inside? When they learned that films titled *Child Robbers* and *The Female Highwaymen* were being shown, these citizens demanded that local officials keep children out of nickelodeons or, better yet, close the theaters so that no one saw such "trash."

One of the first calls for censorship was heard in Chicago. There were over one hundred nickelodeons in the city by 1907, and more than one hundred thousand tickets were sold each day. The editor at the *Chicago Tribune* spoke for many when he said that the influence of nickelodeons was "wholly vicious" and that "there is no voice raised to defend the majority of five cent theatres because they can not be defended. They are hopelessly bad."[2] Censorship, in his opinion, was the only solution.

Other citizens in other cities quickly joined the cry for banning films. Shortly after that, laws were enacted to protect Americans from movies that were thought to lower the public's morals. Chicago, for example, passed a law declaring that nothing obscene, inhuman, indecent, or antireligious could be shown. All films coming into the city were to be viewed by a panel of censors, in this case policemen, who had the absolute power to decide what would be shown and what would be banned.

Needless to say, motion picture companies were not happy about having their films eliminated even before the public could see them. The Mutual Film Corporation decided to challenge a local ordinance in court. Its case, *Mutual Film Corporation* v. *Industrial Commission of Ohio* reached the Supreme Court. Here the film company argued that movies should have the same freedom of expression that other media—books, newspapers, and magazines—were enjoying.

The Supreme Court didn't agree. In 1915, the justices ruled that films were not like other media. Movies, in the Supreme Court's opinion at that time, were not seeking to provide information as were newspapers and books. The justices said that "the exhibition of moving pictures is business pure and simple . . . conducted for profit."[3] Films, therefore, could be censored as much as any community wished.

With the Supreme Court behind them, city councils then began drafting ordinances for controlling what was shown on local screens. Shortly after that, such ordinances were being considered in more than thirty states.

The demand for censorship got even louder in the 1920s, especially after sound was added to films. Script writers, many of whom were former novelists or magazine writers who were used to being able to say what they wanted, provided some pretty lively—some said shocking—dialogue. Not only did many parents cringe at the very thought of their children hearing such words, parents were afraid children who considered movie stars heroes would begin to say the same things.

65

Movies were a popular form of entertainment for young and old in the early 1900s.

A Code Is Established

When worried parents threatened to boycott theaters, movie producers decided that they had to set some standards or lose their audience. As a result, a Production Code Administration was started in the 1930s.

This code was based on three principles. First, no film should threaten the morals of a community. Therefore, movies were to show crime and sin as worthy only of punishment and contempt, and no criminal was to be shown in such a way that he or she might gain any sympathy from the audience. Second, films were supposed to encourage proper standards of behavior. This meant that bad guys could not win anything of value, and children couldn't get the upper hand no matter how clever or cute they might be. And third, rules and laws were not to be ridiculed. Ever.

Although most film producers followed the code, local leaders and concerned citizens weren't willing to take any chances that an objectionable film might appear in their city. By the mid-1930s, most movies had to pass at least two censors before they could be shown—local, and sometimes state, censoring boards, which made recommendations about licenses that granted operators the right to show films, and the Legion of Decency, a movie review group set up by the Catholic Church.

If censors thought a film was basically all right, except for a few "bad" parts, these men and women had the power to demand that such scenes be eliminated. Few theater managers dared to show any film that wasn't approved or "improved" by censors. They feared angering the public and losing their audiences.

Filmmakers Fight Censorship

Although movie producers were willing to accept censor-ship for a while, this didn't mean that they would accept it forever. As book and magazine publishers became bolder in what they produced, there was a demand for more realistic films. By the late 1940s, production code rules seemed old-fashioned, and moviemakers chafed at the lack of freedom to tell a story the way they saw fit.

In 1948, the Supreme Court heard a case about busi-ness practices of film companies that eventually led to the freedom moviemakers wanted. For many years, movie companies not only decided what films were made, they also owned the vast majority of theaters in America, and these theaters showed only company films. The Supreme Court ruled that this procedure gave view-ers few choices, and as a result, it was an unfair business practice. The justices ordered the movie companies to sell their theaters. The Supreme Court also indicated that it now considered films to be a form of communica-tion, reversing its opinion in the *Mutual Film* case.

Many new theater owners, free to pick and choose what they showed, decided to run foreign as well as do-mestic films. One of these foreign films, *The Miracle*, caused an uproar. The movie told a story about a dis-turbed young woman who became pregnant. She was convinced that Saint Joseph was the father of her child, and most of the film dwelled on the scorn and mistreat-ment the young woman endured because of this belief. *The Miracle* was first brought into New York City by Joseph Burstyn, who wanted to show the film in his theater.

After local censors viewed it, they gave the film their approval. However, not everyone was happy with the censors' decision. The Legion of Decency called the film "blasphemous" and condemned it. State censors were so upset when they saw the film—they called it "sacrilegious"—they wanted to take away Burstyn's license to operate a theater. Burstyn then turned to the courts for protection.

In 1952, *Burstyn* v. *Wilson* reached the Supreme Court. Because films were now considered a form of communication, they were protected by the First Amendment. As a result, it was as difficult to censor a film as it would be to censor a book or newspaper. The Supreme Court said that the state couldn't automatically ban a movie because one or two censors found it sacrilegious. The justices also pointed out that the word "sacrilegious," like "obscene," didn't mean the same thing to all people. This didn't mean that a film couldn't be banned, but the Supreme Court made it very clear that censors would have to have very powerful arguments for doing so. In addition, the justices added, each film under attack was entitled to its day in court.

Heartened by the Supreme Court's decision, other theater owners began to challenge state laws that established local and state censors. One by one, state supreme courts found the laws unconstitutional. Now movie producers realized that they had the right to tell a story in any manner they wished, and films became more realistic.

But producers were afraid that new censorship laws might replace the old, and they decided to try to devise a system that would preserve the freedom to produce what they wanted for a variety of different audiences and somehow alert the public about a film's contents to avoid offending anyone. The result was a code whereby each film received a rating. This way viewers could determine which films contained violent or sexually explicit scenes—called "x-rated" then—and which films were deemed suitable for children.

Although the code had flaws and had to be revised several times, it laid the groundwork for the system we have today. Films are now rated "G," all ages admitted, "PG," all ages admitted but parental guidance suggested, "PG-13," all viewers admitted but parental guidance strongly recommended for anyone under thirteen years of age, "R," anyone under seventeen years of age must be accompanied by a parent or guardian, and "NC-17," no one under the age of seventeen will be admitted.

This system provides protection for children as well as for controversial films and, in general, seems acceptable to most people. This doesn't mean that demands for censorship of films have completely died out. Nor does it mean that no controversy over films will develop in the future—for few films please everyone and the issue of free speech is involved.

7

Radio and Television— Who Controls the Airwaves?

A door, squeaking and grinding on its hinges, opened ever so slowly, breaking a long silence. Next, a man's loud, wicked laugh was heard. These spooky sound effects opened every episode of one of the most popular radio programs in the 1940s, "The Shadow." Millions of listeners tuned in each week to hear Lamont Cranston, the program's hero, outwit evil men and women.

This program was only one of dozens of serials that had loyal followers then. Many women listened to "Stella Dallas" as she helped friends and family members solve their problems. Children listened to "Story Time" or half-hour westerns in which the Lone Ranger or Gene Autry regularly rounded up horse thieves and cattle rustlers.

Radio Broadcasters Seek Controls

Unlike novelists, magazine publishers, and movie producers, who wanted no regulation by the government, radio broadcasters sought regulation as early as 1920, only months after the first radio station, KDKA in Pittsburgh, Pennsylvania, went on the air. Broadcasters did this because frequencies are limited, and without organization and control over who was going to broadcast at what frequency and when, station owners feared chaos.

To regulate radio broadcasting, Congress established the Federal Radio Commission in 1927. This act enabled the commission to set frequencies and hours for 732 radio stations on the air then. The commission did not regulate what was broadcast, though. In fact, there was little concern over programming content since most of these stations were owned by radio manufacturers who hoped to encourage more people to buy radios by broadcasting noncontroversial entertainment. More than six hundred of these stations ran educational programs. Other stations were supported by universities or churches, and neither group, like radio manufacturers, wanted to be associated with offensive broadcasts.

By 1934, Congress decided to create a new agency, the Federal Communications Commission (FCC) to control all forms of telecommunications—radio, telegraph, and telephone. (When television was invented, it was put under the jurisdiction of the FCC as well.) Before 1934, control over the various forms of telecommunications had been scattered throughout several agencies, and the results were confusion and inefficiency. The new commission, whose members were appointed by the president of the United States, was authorized to extend or reduce communications services, license stations and operators, assign frequencies, regulate rates—telephone charges, for instance, or today, monthly cable rates—and monitor any telecommunication operation to make sure it obeyed FCC rules. Program content was up to station owners, many of whom joined the National Association of Broadcasters. These broadcasters followed the code established in 1927, which said broadcasters would serve the public.

But soon an argument took place over what "serve the public" meant. Universities thought it meant broadcasting lectures and offering college credit to listeners. Other station owners thought it meant broadcasting programs to entertain as well as selling advertising time on the air to make a profit. In short, another argument over what should be said was in progress.

The idea of putting ads on the air, first suggested by American Telephone and Telegraph, had many supporters. These supporters believed that there was nothing wrong with companies buying time "to talk to the public and at the same time tell the public something it would like to hear."[1] Besides, ads could bring in lots of money for the stations.

Opponents of radio ads called the idea "mercenary" and "offensive." Secretary of Commerce Herbert Hoover, who later would become president, said that it was "inconceivable that we should allow so great a possibility for service . . . to be drowned in advertising chatter."[2]

Nevertheless, American Telephone and Telegraph went ahead with its advertising program on its station

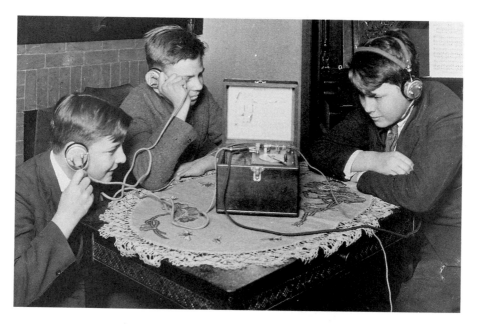

Some of the first radios were little more than wooden boxes with headsets. Favorite children's programs then included mysteries and westerns.

WEAF. Shortly after that, a Queensboro Corporation paid $50 for a ten-minute spot to sell its housing. Within three weeks, Queensboro had sold properties worth $127,000 as a result of the ad. Eventually, advertising on the radio became so successful, companies were clamoring for air time.

When choosing when to run their ads, business owners looked for programs that had the biggest audiences so they could reach the most people possible. Interest in mysteries and westerns ran high, so advertisers chose to support these productions over concerts and lectures, which had small audiences.

But each radio program could only have so many sponsors, and the hours each station could broadcast were limited. Radio stations seeking ever higher profits then cut educational broadcasts and scheduled more quiz programs, variety shows, and comedies in their places. Suddenly, what was being said on the radio was strongly influenced by advertisers.

Radio Loses Its Audience

Although radio programs were one of the main forms of entertainment from 1930 to 1950, interest in these programs began to wither away when television became popular. As more and more people purchased TV sets, advertisers decided to spend their money in television studios. From then on, radio stations could no longer afford to run traditional programs with stars who wanted big salaries, so stations switched their format. They began to play records. These programs were inexpensive to produce, and they became quite popular.

In the late 1980s and early 1990s, some radio stations

decided to run talk shows, a format which had been used successfully before, to increase the number of listeners. Although most talk show hosts expected self-censorship, that is, guests would choose their words carefully, a few stations ran programs that were deliberately designed to shock. These shock shows included controversial topics few people would discuss in polite company, especially unusual sexual behavior.

One program in particular, Howard Stern's, enraged some listeners, and they complained to the FCC. Critics said that Stern not only broadcast sexually explicit and offensive material regularly, which was not illegal, but he did this during hours when such material was supposed to be off-limits, six in the morning until midnight. Irate listeners urged the FCC to take away the station's license.

The FCC levied a fine of $600,000 against the company that employed Stern, but it did not revoke the station's license. This was a record fine, and many supporters of First Amendment rights for radio broadcasters were appalled. Stern's supporters argued that radio programs should have more freedom and that time restrictions should not apply.

So far, the U.S. Supreme Court has not granted this freedom. It has refused to do so because, unlike buying books or attending rock concerts where one knows what the contents are like, listeners may be subjected to language they find offensive if controls are not in place. Justice John Stevens said, "Because the broadcast audience is constantly tuning in and out, prior warnings [such as those used on movies] cannot completely protect the listener . . . from unexpected program content. To say that one may avoid further offense by turning off the radio when he hears indecent language is like saying that the remedy for assault is to run away after the first blow. . . . That option does not avoid a harm that has already taken place."[3]

Supreme Court justices also considered the fact that listeners were in their homes when confronted with such language. Stevens said, "Indecent material presented over the airwaves confronts the citizen . . . in the privacy of the home, where the individual's right to be left alone plainly outweighs the First Amendment rights of an intruder."[4] In addition, there were young children in many homes who listened to the radio during the day, and they needed protection from such material, an important issue that would face television producers as well.

Television Enters the Picture

Like radio broadcasters, television producers agreed to serve the public interest, and by 1952, producers had established a voluntary TV code to set standards for what viewers saw in their homes. At first, many of the programs broadcast were very similar to those once heard on radio—westerns, quiz shows, comedies, and variety acts. In fact, many of TV's first stars were former radio celebrities, like the Lone Ranger, who continued to play their old parts. But competition between the television networks soon became intense, and when producers learned that violent programs drew large audiences, more and more programs included shootings, muggings, bombings, and car crashes. By 1960, violence on TV had become very common.

Although violent acts were presented regularly in books and films then, many viewers believed that such

77

acts portrayed on TV were especially dangerous. As one critic said, "TV is present in almost all homes and children have unregulated access to it. Not only does the combination of sight and sound have particularly potent influence, but TV does not have the built-in protections of print media. To 'witness' violence in a book you must be able to read the book. . . . Violence in film . . . has a 'box office barrier.' An adult must take the child to the . . . theater. But none of this is so with television. Even the preschool child can experience murder, muggings, rape, and robbery by turning on the TV set . . . which any two-year-old knows how to do."[5]

In 1961, a National Commission on Violence was formed. After listening to hours of testimony by experts about the effects of watching violence on television, the commission claimed that violent television programs contributed to the rising tide of violence in America. Just as there was debate about the effect of violent movies on children, there was considerable discussion over this announcement as well. And the discussion continues even today. Many studies have been made over the years about the possible connection of violence in the media and violence in society. To date, no definite correlation has been made.

Television executives in 1961 didn't think that the conclusion reached by the National Commission on Violence was accurate, but they still promised to cut back on violent episodes, hoping to calm would-be censors. However, the executives were well aware that many Americans wanted violent programs. They also knew that the larger the audiences were, the more programs could charge per minute for advertising. Therefore, although television executives promised to limit violence on the television set, few made a serious effort to do so.

Advertisers Come Under Fire

When TV executives failed to curb violent episodes or sexually explicit material, some irate citizens took action. They wrote to the programs' sponsors and threatened to boycott their products.

For instance, one housewife in Michigan, Terry Rakolta, began a letter-writing campaign to pressure advertisers to stop sponsoring "Married . . . With Children." Then she encouraged others to do the same. Although only one sponsor decided to stop advertising on this program, it was still a victory for Rakolta, for she had shown how powerful angry viewers could become.[6] A few months later, advertisers, afraid of future letter-writing campaigns and boycotts, refused to support a program called "Crimes of Passion II," and some advertisers began to withdraw ads from any programs viewers might find offensive.[7]

At the same time viewers were attacking advertisers for the programs they sponsored, other viewers began to attack some ads. Liquor and cigarette companies found themselves under siege in all media by health-conscious groups who fought hard to take away these advertisers' opportunity to talk about their products.

Action for Children's Television (ACT) pressured television producers to refuse to accept candy companies as sponsors for children's programs. Sugary foods, ACT argued, caused tooth decay, and too much sugar in one's diet resulted in poor nutrition as well. ACT members noted that in one seven-hour period of children's programs

79

Three-year-old Dorothy Jean Edge is seated before a radio-phonograph-television set her father built in 1947. Note the size of the screen.

appearing on a typical Saturday, sixty-seven commercials for candy or highly sweetened products—sugar-coated cereals, for example—had appeared. ACT saw no value in stuffing kids with Kit-Kats, Pop Tarts, Twinkies, or Ring-Dings, and it insisted that such ads be eliminated. Eventually the number of such commercials was reduced due to ACT's campaign.

Other advertisers were taken to court over false claims. To avoid trouble, soup companies suddenly stopped putting glass marbles in the bottom of soup bowls shown in commercials to make vegetables rise to the top, giving a false impression of how many carrots and peas were in the broth. Others chose their words more carefully, stopping short of promising miracles if only viewers would use their products.

Public Television Begins Broadcasting

In 1952, the FCC granted permission for stations that wanted to produce educational programs to use a special waveband, UHF. Because these stations decided not to accept advertising, most had little money with which to work, and the majority had to rely on contributions from viewers for funding. One station in Los Angeles was so short of funds, it could only afford to broadcast one hour a day. Private foundations came to these stations' rescue, and eventually the National Educational Television network was established.

In 1967, the federal government believed that educational television was so important, it voted to help fund the system. Educational TV was reorganized and renamed. Known from then on as the Public Broadcasting System (PBS), it was supposed to have complete freedom

81

to run whatever programs the producers thought should appear. Among its many dramas and concerts, PBS also ran documentaries on current events, including the war in Vietnam. Some of these documentaries criticized America's role in the war, and this infuriated government officials. PBS was told to stop showing such programs, or it would lose its federal funds. PBS broadcasters refused to censor programs that offended the government, and officials retaliated by cutting funding, just as they had threatened to do.

The network then had to look about for other sources of income. It held fund drives among viewers and turned to corporations for support. This has caused alarm among some viewers who believe that sponsors may have some control over the programs.

Viewers' Choices Expand

In the early 1950s, satellite dishes and cable networks made their debut. Both used special equipment to pick up broadcast signals from many stations, and both greatly enlarged the number of choices available for viewers, especially those subscribing to cable television. Although cable subscriptions grew slowly in the beginning, more than forty-five million homes receive cable broadcasts today. These networks not only offer traditional programs carried by the major networks, they also offer continuous news programs, adult education classes, and local programs that show events happening in one's community. The number of channels available not only gives viewers more choices, it also gives more producers an opportunity to air their views—a right protected by the First Amendment.

8

Speaking Out for Change

On December 16, 1965, thirteen-year-old Mary Beth Tinker, her fifteen-year-old brother, John, and a friend, Chris Eckhardt, wore black armbands to their schools in Des Moines, Iowa. They wanted to show, through a peaceful means, their opposition to American involvement in Vietnam, and this seemed the best way to do it. But their principals were afraid that the sight of the bands might cause a disturbance in the classrooms, and the children were told to remove them as soon as they entered their schools. When the Tinkers and Eckhardt refused to do so, they were suspended.

The teenagers believed that their First Amendment rights had been violated, and they sought help from the Iowa Civil Liberties Union. The union agreed to represent the students, and it filed a petition on their behalf in the district court of the United States. However, although

Mary Beth Tinker was suspended from school for wearing a black armband, a symbol of opposition to the United States' involvement in Vietnam. Here, surrounded by supporters, she waits with her mother for her first hearing in court.

the court agreed that the armbands were a form of symbolic speech, the court decided in favor of the school district, believing that the armbands might cause a disturbance.

The Iowa Civil Liberties Union decided to appeal this decision. The union turned first to the U.S. Court of Appeals in the Eighth Circuit, and when it lost there, the union petitioned the U.S. Supreme Court to hear the case, which it agreed to do.

In 1969, the Supreme Court announced its decision. By a vote of 7 to 2, the justices said that the armbands were protected by the First Amendment, even if school officials thought they might cause a ruckus. Justice Abe Fortas wrote, "The district court concluded that the action of the school authorities was reasonable because it was based on the fear of a disturbance from the wearing of armbands. . . . Any departure from absolute regimentation may inspire fear. Any word spoken in class, in the lunchroom or on the campus that [differs] from the view of another person may start an argument or cause a disturbance. But our Constitution says we must take this risk . . . and our history says it is this sort of hazardous freedom—this kind of openness—that is the basis of our national strength."[1]

Early Protesters

The Tinkers and Eckhardt were only three of many protesters in American history who sought change. Long before America gained its independence, colonists protested against England's taxation policy by burning British proclamations and marching down cobblestone streets. When the king failed to change his ways, many

85

colonists decided to change their government, and shortly after, they declared their independence.

The belief that Americans had the right to peacefully protest against their leaders' actions or challenge laws only grew stronger after the Revolutionary War. Because the First Amendment forbids Congress to limit free speech, and later the Fourteenth Amendment stopped states from doing so, political leaders weren't supposed to be able to stop criticism or protests that threatened their power or tried to force them to change their policies. This didn't keep them from trying to do so, though.

Protesting Against Policies Over the Years

One of the first attempts of the federal government to limit protest occurred in 1798. Federalists, who were in control of the government then, were enraged by verbal attacks by Republicans. Believing they could not win re-election if they could not stop the steady stream of Republican criticism, the Federalists passed the Sedition Act. This act, which was to expire just after the next election, made it illegal to defame a political leader.

Although they were under great pressure to keep quiet after the law passed, Republicans increased their attacks, and they added limiting freedom of speech to their long list of "crimes" committed by the Federalists. When some Republican supporters were arrested for violating the Sedition Act, Americans turned against the Federalists, and they voted this party out of office in the next election.

That is, men voted out the Federalists. Women couldn't cast a ballot then. Although women grumbled over the inequity, they did not begin to organize for suffrage, the right to vote, until 1848, and the movement was very small then. By the early 1900s, however, the suffrage movement had grown enormously, and women were routinely petitioning the government for equal rights. When their pleas were ignored by elected officials who believed they didn't need to concern themselves with people who couldn't vote, the women turned to tactics designed to draw attention to their cause, increase their number of supporters, and pressure the government into granting suffrage.

Suffragettes made full use of the First Amendment. They spoke before as many audiences as possible all across the nation, lobbied congressmen, organized large rallies and parades, and arranged to have their events covered by many newspapers. Some women even picketed the White House.

Eventually the majority of Americans, including many male voters, supported the suffragettes. These people pressured federal and state legislators to do the same. As a result, an amendment granting women the right to vote was finally passed by Congress and ratified by three-fourths of the state legislatures by 1920.

Because the women's tactics had been so successful, they were copied by other groups over the years that also wanted to change the government's policies. These groups included thousands of people dedicated to ending racial segregation in America in the early 1960s. Like the suffragettes, members of this movement lobbied congressmen and held marches and demonstrations to draw attention to their plight.

Not everyone wanted African Americans to have equality, and in some cities, local authorities did all they could to prevent any demonstration that might arouse some sympathy for the protesters. For example, police refused to give African Americans permits to march in some cities. Police had the right to do this if they believed that a parade was likely to tie up traffic. But denying a permit just to hurt the marchers' cause limited free speech, and African Americans believed that their extraordinarily large number of refusals was nothing more than an attempt to deny them their First Amendment rights.

Frustrated by the permit system, many African Americans decided to march without permission, and this sometimes resulted in violent confrontations. In Birmingham, Alabama, for instance, the police commissioner routinely denied African Americans permits to march. On May 2, 1962, five hundred high school students decided to hold a parade anyway. They were arrested as were other African-American students who organized a sympathy demonstration for their jailed friends the next day—after the sympathizers were pelted with bottles and brickbats. On May 4, more than two thousand demonstrators marched to protest the arrests and violence. This time officers turned fire hoses and police dogs loose on defenseless men and women.

These events were televised all across the nation. The violent scenes shocked and appalled many Americans, and they also raised lots of support for the marchers, the opposite effect of what the police were trying to achieve.

The violence in Birmingham, coupled with the murder of several civil rights workers in Mississippi, terrified many of the movement's supporters, black and white.

Civil rights protesters often used marches to call attention to their cause, a peaceful action with a long history that is protected by the First Amendment. Martin Luther King, Jr., is pictured fifth from the left in the front row.

Fear became a very powerful censor, and some would-be protesters were just too frightened to speak out.

But no matter how hard opponents of civil rights tried, they could not silence everyone, and the dignity and dedication of the leaders of the movement and their persistent plea for simple justice won over most Americans and many government leaders. Old legislation to end segregation was enforced, and new laws were passed to give African Americans more rights.

Civil rights demonstrations had barely ended when protesters who wanted American troops to withdraw from Vietnam took to the streets to build support for their position. Although demonstrators used many old tactics, including a massive march on Washington, D.C. by more than thirty thousand people, to pressure the government into changing its policies, antiwar demonstrators also used some new methods to gain attention. These actions included setting the American flag on fire. This was the most controversial of the new tactics, and it was deeply offensive to many Americans. But like the wearing of armbands, this was a form of symbolic speech and therefore protected by the First Amendment. As opposition to the war increased, in part due to the demonstrations, the government withdrew American forces from Vietnam.

Demonstrators who want to change some of our laws today march or hold rallies. Antiabortion groups, for example, often hold rallies to win supporters for their cause. Sometimes, opponents trying to hinder a movement heckle speakers to try to make them stop talking, or they shout to drown out speakers. These actions, like instilling fear, are attempts at censorship.

Socialist and Communist Protests

Although most protesters wanted only to change a particular policy, some socialists and communists hoped to bring about drastic change in America's economy and change the government itself. As a result, these groups were treated differently from other protesters.

The Social Democratic Party of America was founded in 1901. This party was led by Eugene Debs. Debs was deeply upset by the enormous wealth and power some industrial leaders were accumulating then and the extreme poverty in which many workers lived. He urged workers, who, he said, were slaves under the present system, to unite and fight for better wages and working conditions. The Social Democratic Party also believed that workers, not industrialists, should own businesses and that private wealth should be abolished.[2]

The very thought of such drastic change frightened many Americans, and they wanted the socialists silenced. Their chance to do so occurred shortly after America entered World War I, when Congress passed the Espionage Act of 1917. This act, among other things, made it illegal to interfere with drafting men to fight.

The leaders of the Socialist party ignored the act. Debs and most of his followers believed that the war would be run by businessmen and fought by poor workers. Therefore, Debs and other officers of the party encouraged workers to refuse to fight. When Charles Schenck, general secretary of the party, distributed fifteen thousand leaflets to young men urging them to refuse to serve in the armed services, he was arrested,

91

tried, and found guilty of violating the Espionage Act. He claimed he was denied his right of free speech.

When Schenck appealed his case, the Supreme Court upheld his conviction because it believed Schenck's pamphlets had presented a dangerous threat that the government had a right to stop. The Supreme Court said, "The most stringent protection of free speech would not protect a man in falsely shouting fire in a theatre, and causing a panic. . . . The question . . . is whether the words used are used in such circumstances and are of such a nature as to create a clear and present danger."[3] In this case, the Supreme Court said that Schenck had presented a serious threat to a country at war by urging its young men not to fight.

Schenck was not the only socialist arrested during the war. Debs and at least five other officers also spent time in prison. Without its leaders, the organization began to falter, and members fought among themselves. Eventually, about one third of the socialists joined the American Communist Party.

Although the Communist party in the Soviet Union became quite powerful after World War I ended, it wasn't until the end of World War II, when Soviet dictators took control of many countries in Europe and began eyeing more territory, that Americans really felt threatened by the new superpower. As a result, some government officials began to persecute American communists because they believed these communists were spying for the Soviets and preparing to take over the U.S. government by force. Congress passed laws that took away many rights from communists in the early

Eugene Debs, leader of the Socialist Party, encouraged members of a large crowd in Canton, Ohio, not to support America's entry into World War I. He was arrested shortly after he gave this speech.

1950s and made it nearly impossible for them to demonstrate in public to gain supporters.

One of the first free speech cases to be heard under the new laws is known as *Dennis* v. *United States.* Eugene Dennis, a communist, was arrested when he made plans to talk to others about overthrowing the United States government. Dennis insisted that he had the right to talk about this because all ideas can be discussed in a democracy. He challenged communist control laws but was sent to prison, anyway. His sentence was upheld by the Supreme Court. The justices said that advocating "the overthrow of the government by force and violence is certainly a substantial enough [reason] for the government to limit speech."[4]

Believing there were many communists at work, Senator Joseph McCarthy of Wisconsin started a witch-hunt. Suspects, which McCarthy seemed to find everywhere, especially in the government and in schools, were dragged before communist hearings boards. Just to be brought before such boards was enough to ruin the careers of teachers and textbook writers, and many people began to watch what they said or wrote very carefully.

By the late 1950s, the public had had enough of the persecutions. Hundreds of Americans had been hurt when accused of being communists, and there was no proof that American communists were about to overthrow the government. As a result, the Supreme Court began to grant greater freedom to communists, including the right to speak out and organize as a political party.

Senator Joseph McCarthy feared communists, and he was determined to deny them any right to organize or speak out in America.

Self-publishers Working for Change

Not all groups seeking change are large enough to hold huge rallies or organize parades, nor do all groups wish to do so. Usually these organizations rely on speaking before sympathetic audiences or the distribution of self-published material to build support. But even though every American has the right to publish whatever he or she wants, distribution can be regulated, and this has sometimes placed limits on free speech.

One of the most common methods of handing out self-published literature is to stand on a street corner and give papers to anyone passing by. In the past, many city officials have forbidden such activity because they believed that littering might result. In some cases, permits were required by anyone who wanted to pass out papers. Because local officials had the power to deny permits, they also had enormous power over the self-publisher. They could, if they wished to do so, prohibit anyone with whom they disagreed from distributing materials.

In the late 1930s, several people challenged antilittering laws that limited their right to distribute material. The Supreme Court struck down such laws because the justices believed that the threat of littering was not great enough to limit such a precious freedom as sharing information. Without the right to distribute, the justices said, what good is the right to publish? Besides, the justices added, "There are obvious methods of preventing littering. Amongst these is the punishment of those who actually throw papers on the streets."[5]

The Supreme Court was also asked to examine regulations that required people who went door to door to

96

distribute material to have a permit. The Supreme Court declared such laws unconstitutional. Justice Black said that "freedom to distribute information to every citizen wherever he desires to receive it is so clearly vital to preservation of a free society that (aside from reasonable regulations dealing with the time and manner of distribution) it must be fully preserved."[6]

In short, no city could demand that a self-publisher obtain a permit before distributing material on the sidewalk or in the neighborhood. On the other hand, reasonable restrictions are allowed. No one can go door to door at four o'clock in the morning, nor can anyone hand out fliers in the middle of a busy interstate highway. However, "reasonable," like "obscene," doesn't mean the same thing to all people, and conflicts over distribution are likely to occur in the future.

9

Words of Malice and Violence

Brooks Fain committed suicide on August 30, 1992, only a few days before he would have started classes as a high school freshman. For months, classmates had been taunting him, accusing him of lewd behavior. When his tormentors couldn't shout at him in person, they called his home and left obscene messages on the family's answering machine. Brooks's good name and reputation were ruined, and his friends abandoned him, one by one. Eventually he saw death as the only escape from the pain and humiliation he felt.

After Brooks's death, his tormentors—who said the rumors were just a prank—were arrested and charged with making obscene phone calls. Other charges were considered as well.[1]

While the First Amendment protects many forms of

speech, it does not protect lies and mean-spirited words said only to ruin someone's reputation so others will hold that person in contempt. If false statements are said in the presence of others, the insulted person can sue for slander. If such statements are printed, the person affected can sue for libel.

Libel law has two sets of standards, one for the famous, another for the rest of society. In general, average citizens have been given more protection by the courts than public figures, such as politicians and entertainers, who by the very nature of their work draw attention to themselves and must expect some criticism. Most citizens need only to prove that the statements in question are false and that they have caused harm, a lost job, for instance, or lost social standing, to win a case. Politicians must prove much more, as the following case illustrates.

The Sullivan Case—with Malice in Mind?

On March 29, 1960, the *New York Times* carried an ad designed to raise money for civil rights groups. The ad described incidents nonviolent protesters encountered as a "wave of terror" in which marchers faced "truckloads of police armed with shotguns and tear gas."[2] The ad was signed by sixty-four well-known leaders.

When L. B. Sullivan read the ad, he was very upset, for it exaggerated how the police reacted to the demonstrators. Sullivan had been the Commissioner of Public Affairs in Montgomery, Alabama, when the demonstrations described took place, and he had been responsible for the police department. He feared that everyone would believe the ad and hold him in contempt as a result. Sullivan then decided to sue the *Times* for libel to protect his reputation.

During the trial, Sullivan's lawyer proved that the ad contained errors, and he insisted that the editors at the *Times* had been very careless because they had not checked the ad's information before running it. Their carelessness had caused Sullivan great embarrassment, the lawyer added, and he deserved to be compensated. The jury agreed and awarded the former commissioner $500,000.

As would be expected, the *Times* appealed the case. Although the State Supreme Court of Alabama upheld the decision, in 1964 the U.S. Supreme Court unanimously reversed it. The Supreme Court ruled in *New York Times* v. *Sullivan* that Sullivan had to show that the ad was false *and* that the publishers were aware of this fact before they ran the ad in order for Sullivan to claim that the paper was careless. Since the ad was signed by sixty-four experts, the *Times* had every reason to assume the piece was accurate. The justices said that Sullivan also had to show that the ad was run with malice in mind, that is, the editors wanted to hurt him, a fact that wasn't proved during the trial.

This case established the libel rules, especially those relating to politicians, that are followed today. Leaders must show that malice is involved before they can win a suit. This difficult step prevents political leaders from stopping the press every time it criticizes them by threatening to sue the paper. On the other hand, the malice requirement does not prevent leaders from protecting their reputations from anyone who really publishes lies out of spite or hatred.

Fighting Words

Besides limiting libelous words, the Supreme Court has also limited another form of harmful speech, "fighting words." The first such case began in 1942 when a man known simply as Chaplinsky handed out leaflets about his religious beliefs on a street corner in Rochester, New Hampshire. A crowd formed, and Chaplinsky berated anyone who did not believe as he did. A marshal, sensing trouble in the making, told Chaplinsky to watch his words. Shortly after that, a scuffle broke out, and Chaplinsky was led away to the local jail.

On his way, Chaplinsky argued with the marshal, calling him "a God damned racketeer and a damned fascist."[3] Swearing at the marshal, or anyone else, in a public place violated New Hampshire law. When Chaplinsky was charged, he claimed that his right of free speech had been violated.

The Supreme Court, which heard *Chaplinsky* v. *New Hampshire* in 1942, didn't agree. Justice Murphy spoke for the Supreme Court in its unanimous decision. "There are certain well-defined and narrowly limited classes of speech [which are not protected]. These include the lewd and obscene, the profane, the libelous, and the insulting or 'fighting' words."[4] These words, Murphy added, have no social value. Not only do they not help express ideas worth considering, they could cause someone to fight, an activity society does not encourage.

Another famous "fighting words" case, *Feiner* v. *New*

York, began in 1949 when Irving Feiner, a college student, addressed a crowd of blacks and whites on a street corner in Syracuse, New York. Feiner was unhappy with a number of public officials and their policies, and he lost little time telling seventy to eighty people how he felt. He called the American Legion "a Nazi Gestapo" and the mayor of Syracuse "a champagne-sipping bum who does not speak out for the Negro people." He then told the African Americans in his audience "to rise up in arms and fight for their rights."[5]

Some listeners were becoming pretty upset, and one man threatened to pull Feiner from the speaker's stand. Someone called the police, claiming that trouble was brewing, and officers rushed to the scene where they asked Feiner—twice—to stop speaking. He refused to do so. When people began to push toward him, the police arrested him to avoid a fight.

Feiner was tried for breaking a New York ordinance that made it illegal for people to use offensive language in public or cause others to breach the peace (fight). Feiner argued that this regulation took away his right to free speech. The court didn't agree. Feiner then appealed his case, which eventually reached the Supreme Court. In a 6 to 3 decision, the Court upheld Feiner's conviction in 1951 because his words were capable of causing a ruckus.

Threatening Words

Besides limiting fighting words, the courts have also put limits on threatening words. One of the best-known cases of this type involved the Ku Klux Klan, an organization started shortly after the Civil War ended in 1865,

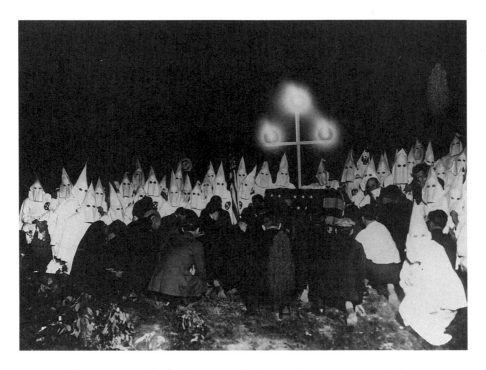

The Ku Klux Klan has long preached hatred toward Jews, Catholics, and immigrants. Members used to wear robes and masks to hide their identity and often met in isolated spots at night to plan activities.

which preached hatred toward African Americans, Jews, and immigrants. In 1964, Klan member Clarence Brandenburg, gave a shocking speech on television. Brandenburg said that "niggers should be returned to Africa and the Jews should be returned to Israel" and that if the government wouldn't stand up for the rights of whites, the Klan "might have to take revenge."[6]

Brandenburg was arrested shortly after for his threatening remarks and convicted of inciting violence. He appealed his case, *Brandenburg* v. *Ohio*, to the Supreme Court, and in 1969, the justices reversed his conviction. The Supreme Court said that Brandenburg's speech was not illegal even if it was repulsive and he talked about using violence. "The line, [the Supreme Court] said should be drawn only against speech that advocates lawless action when it is also likely to lead to such action."[7] Since there was no violence involved, Brandenburg could not be punished. If Klan members had begun to take revenge though, Brandenburg's case would have had a different ending.

Protecting Hateful Speech

Although members of the Klan could easily upset audiences, no group appeared to be able to do it better than the American Nazi Party. This group, like the Klan, promoted hatred of African Americans and Jews. Members wore swastikas just as Hitler's followers in Germany had, and this symbol was a revolting reminder of the horrors suffered by more than six million Jews who died at the hands of the Nazis during World War II.

In the spring of 1977, a Chicago-based Nazi group

decided to march in nearby Skokie, Illinois. Skokie had a large number of Jewish citizens, including three thousand immigrants who had barely managed to survive Hitler's death camps. The very thought of Nazis marching down the streets proudly displaying their swastikas was more than the citizens of Skokie, Jewish or not, could stand. The Nazis reveled in the controversy, for it greatly upset those they hated the most.

The citizens of Skokie tried to stop the Nazis from marching and speaking by requiring parade permits, which included expensive insurance policies to cover damages if riots erupted. Although this was designed to stop just the Nazis, the permit and insurance policies, which could run as high as $900, eliminated almost everyone who might want to march. Skokie residents also argued that fights might take place. This was reason enough, they said, to stop the hatemongers from making a public appearance.

The American Civil Liberties Union defended the Nazis' right to march. When the case reached the state supreme court, the court said that in a democracy, the Nazis could march and speak out just as everyone else could. The threat of a hostile audience was not an important enough reason to limit free speech. The court reasoned that if the threat of violence was enough to stop them, then every group that had enemies could be silenced by the threat of a fight. Police, the court said, should control the crowds, if necessary.[8]

When the Nazis finally did make their public appearance, they were heavily guarded by policemen. The speakers were greeted by huge, extremely hostile crowds

The words on the signs carried by members of the American Nazi Party would anger many Americans. However, in a democracy, citizens are allowed to voice all ideas, even those that are unpopular.

that shouted so loudly the Nazis' message could not be heard.

Controlling Insulting Words—Speech Codes

In the 1980s, there was a frightening increase in the number of racial incidents on college campuses—name-calling, signs painted on dormitory doors, and threats to African Americans. Some college administrators feared that such ugly incidents seriously undermined the learning environment, and they decided to write speech codes to control what students said on campus.

Administrators at Stanford University in California developed one of the first codes. It forbade students to use words that would insult an individual on the basis of his or her sex, race, color, handicap, religion, sexual orientation, or national and ethnic origin. This greatly expanded the idea of "fighting words." Other universities followed Stanford's example and established speech rules as well.

Critics of the Stanford code reacted immediately. One said that the code was too vague. He wondered if the university would provide a list of forbidden words that should not be said to each student, since not everyone reacted the same way to a particular word. Another said that the code could be twisted around to limit speech no one wanted to stop. And another critic said that the university was trying to take a shortcut to solving a social problem: prejudice. Limiting speech, this critic said, didn't change the feelings behind hateful words, but discussing these feelings might.[9]

Wherever speech codes have been challenged, they have been struck down by the courts as too vague and a violation of the First Amendment. The universities are to be places of learning where the free exchange of ideas can be made—even if not everyone likes the language used to express these ideas.

10

The Right to
Remain Silent

The words "I pledge allegiance to the flag of the United States of America . . ." used to signal the beginning of another school day for children. This pledge was created by a writer at *Youth's Companion,* a children's magazine, in 1892, and it was so well received, many state legislatures required students and teachers to recite the pledge every day as a way to encourage patriotism. Later, some school systems required students to salute the flag as well, a form of symbolic speech, a trend that grew over the coming years.

In 1935, the Minersville, Pennsylvania, school board decided to require a salute. Lillian and William Gobitis and Edmund Wasiewski attended Minersville schools then, and they refused to obey this order. These children were Jehovah's Witnesses, and like all Witnesses, they took the Bible passages that told them not to bow down

Reciting the Pledge of Allegiance and saluting the flag used to be a
daily activity in classrooms all across America.

before images or symbols very seriously. To them, saluting the flag was the same as bowing before it. Such action, according to the children's religious beliefs, meant eternal damnation. When they refused to obey the new regulations, they were expelled from school.

The Gobitises believed their Constitutional rights had been violated, and they went to court. How, they wondered, could a democracy force citizens to say something—even if it was done with a silent motion—that violated their religious beliefs?

At the first hearing, the children and a representative from the national headquarters of the Jehovah's Witnesses convinced the judge that the children's refusal to follow orders was a matter of conscience. The school board, however, would not give up. Everyone, it insisted, was going to recite the pledge and salute the flag.

The board then appealed the case, and when the second court agreed with the first, the board appealed to the U.S. Supreme Court. In 1940, the Supreme Court said, in a vote of 7 to 1, that school boards could demand that students recite the pledge and salute the flag. In order for the nation to be strong, the justices argued, it had to have loyal citizens, and the salute was one method of encouraging loyalty.

Because Witnesses continued to refuse to salute, they were now thought to be disloyal Americans, and they were persecuted all over the country. For example, a mob attacked Witnesses at a Bible meeting in Maryland. In Illinois, a large crowd seized literature from Witnesses who were going door to door and burned their publications. Witnesses were also driven out of cities in Mississippi,

113

Texas, California, Arkansas, and Wyoming, and in some cities they were actually attacked and maimed.[1]

Encouraged by the Gobitis decision, other states passed salute laws, including the state of West Virginia. Once again, Witnesses refused to obey the law, and they were expelled.

Court hearings followed, and another salute case, *West Virginia State Board of Education* v. *Barnette*, reached the Supreme Court in 1943. This time the Supreme Court decided in favor of the children. Persuaded by Justice Robert Jackson, the justices now felt that a great wrong had been committed in the Gobitis case. The state, the Supreme Court said, had no right to force citizens to say anything—aloud or through symbolic speech—that violated their beliefs.

A Test Students Don't Have to Take

Another situation in which children gained the right to remain silent grew out of a testing program developed in the 1970s. At that time, drug use among teenagers was increasing dramatically. A psychologist, Fred Streit, had studied drug addicts, and he developed a summary of what addicts believed about themselves and their families. Streit thought that children who felt the same way about themselves as addicts did would be at risk for taking drugs, and he developed a test, which contained very personal questions, to identify children with similar feelings. Potential addicts identified by the test were to receive counseling designed to keep them away from drugs.

But when the testing program was introduced in Norristown, Pennsylvania, some parents and members of

Lillian Gobitis and her brother, William, were expelled from elementary school when they refused to recite the Pledge of Allegiance.

the American Civil Liberties Union believed that the test violated the children's right to privacy and could cause some serious problems. Students who were thought to be at risk would be identified when they received counseling in school, and this might make them subjects of ridicule. One lawyer for the parents also argued that students might become afraid to express unpopular answers since anything but "normal" answers might mark them as potential addicts. The result, he said, would be that "political dissent, differences of opinion, and open . . . inquiry will be . . . stifled in the very [place] in which they should be protected and encouraged."[2]

When this test was challenged in the U.S. District Court of Eastern Pennsylvania (*Merriken* v. *Cressman*), the judge ordered the school system to stop giving the test, agreeing that it violated the children's right to privacy. However, much to the dismay of some students, the courts have not thrown out tests on reading, writing, or arithmetic. These are not invasions of privacy, no matter how revealing the answers may be, and they do not violate the First Amendment.

In Conclusion

As you have seen, the issue of free speech has caused many arguments among Americans over the last two hundred years. The words that can be printed in newspapers, read in our classrooms, sung in concerts, or given in political rallies have been as hotly contested as the images shown in magazines or on movie and television screens. Even nonverbal speech caused heated debates. And while Americans argued among themselves, judges and Supreme

Court justices weighed the issues, often disagreeing with each other.

Because we are a diverse society with many different beliefs and values, the issue over what can be said will continue to be discussed for many years to come, and each of us should consider the arguments carefully, for much is at stake. Many Americans think that the media is too harsh in its criticism of political leaders. Should reporters continue to have the right to criticize America's leaders anyway? Should children be able to listen to any song they wish or read any book they want? Should any American be allowed to praise the Nazis? Burn the American flag? What do you think?

Notes by Chapter

Chapter 1

1. Nat Hentoff, *Free Speech for Me—But Not for Thee* (New York: HarperCollins, 1992), p. 384.

Chapter 2

1. "Why Johnny Can't Speak," *The Nation* (January 30, 1988), p. 1.

2. *Hazelwood School District* v. *Kuhlmeier*, 484 U.S. 26 (1988).

3. Frank B. Latham, *The Trial of John Peter Zenger, August, 1735* (New York: Franklin Watts, Inc., 1970), p. 49.

4. *New York Times* v. *United States*, 403 U.S. 713 (1971).

Chapter 3

1. Donald J. Rogers, *Banned! Book Censorship in the Schools* (New York: Julian Messner, 1988), pp. 18–19.

2. Olga G. and Edwin P. Hoyt, *Censorship in America* (New York: Seabury Press, 1970), p. 18.

3. Ibid. p. 26.

4. Rogers, p. 42.

Chapter 4

1. Olga G. and Edwin P. Hoyt, *Censorship in America* (New York: Seabury Press, 1970), p. 41.

2. *Hannegan* v. *Esquire*, 327 U.S. 146 (1946).

3. Jethro K. Lieberman, *Free Speech, Free Press, and the Law* (New York: Lothrop, Lee & Shepard Books, 1980), p. 110.

4. "The Supreme Court: Bad News for Smut Peddlers," *Time* (April 1, 1966), p. 57.

Chapter 5

1. Nik Cohn, *Rock From the Beginning* (New York: Stein and Day, 1969), p. 17.

2. "Trigger Happy," *Time* (January 11, 1993), p. 14.

3. John Leland and Linda Buckley, "Number One With a Bullet," *Newsweek* (July 1, 1991), p. 63.

4. Tom Mathews, "Fine Art or Foul?" *Newsweek* (July 2, 1990), p. 52.

5. Robert M. O'Neil, *Classrooms in the Crossfire* (Bloomington, Ind.: Indiana University Press, 1981), p. 84.

Chapter 6

1. Lynn Minton, *Movie Guide for Puzzled Parents* (New York: Delta, 1984), p. 33.

2. Murray Schumach, *The Face on the Cutting Room Floor* (New York: William Morrow & Co., Inc., 1964), p. 16.

3. Olga G. and Edwin P. Hoyt, *Censorship in America* (New York: Seabury Press, 1970), p. 64.

Chapter 7

1. Erik Barnouw, *The Sponsor: Notes on a Modern Potentate* (New York: Oxford University Press, 1978), p. 15.

2. Ibid. p. 15.

3. James Kilpatrick, "Free Speech: Shockjock Pushes Limits on Decency Over the Cliff," *The Milwaukee Journal* (December 29, 1992), p. A-7.

4. Ibid.

5. Kate Moody, *Growing Up on Television: The TV Effect* (New York: Times Books, 1980), p. 78.

6. Richard Zoglin, "Putting a Brake on TV 'Sleaze,'" *Time* (March 20, 1989), p. 51.

7. "Farewell, Trash, Goodbye, Nielsens," *U.S. News and World Report* (May 15, 1989), p. 14.

Chapter 8

1. *Tinker* v. *Des Moines Independent Community School District*, 393 U.S. 503 (1969).

2. Nick Salvatore, *Eugene V. Debs: Citizen and Socialist* (Urbana, Ill.: University of Illinois Press, 1982), p. 293.

3. *Schenck* v. *United States*, 249 U.S. 47 (1919).

4. *Dennis* v. *United States*, 341 U.S. 494 (1951).

5. Jethro K. Lieberman, *Free Speech, Free Press, and the Law* (New York: Lothrop, Lee & Shepard Books, 1980), p. 81.

6. Ibid. pp. 75–76.

Chapter 9

1. Deborah Locke, "Teen Escaped Rumors at School by Taking Life," *Milwaukee Journal* (November 29, 1992), pp. 1, 30.

2. Jethro K. Lieberman, *Free Speech, Free Press, and the Law* (New York: Lothrop, Lee & Shepard Books, 1980), p. 94.

3. Nat Hentoff, *The First Freedom: The Tumultuous History of Free Speech in America* (New York: Delacorte Press, 1980), p. 300.

4. Ibid. p. 301.

5. Lieberman, p. 49.

6. J. Edward Evans, *Freedom of Speech* (Minneapolis: Lerner Publications Co., 1990), p. 50.

7. *Brandenburg* v. *Ohio*, 395 U.S. 444 (1969).

8. Nat Hentoff, *Free Speech for Me—But Not for Thee* (New York: HarperCollins, 1992), p. 255.

9. Ibid. p. 169.

Chapter 10

1. Nat Hentoff, *Free Speech for Me—But Not for Thee* (New York: HarperCollins, 1992), p. 243.

2. Sam and Beryl Epstein, *Kids in Court: The ACLU Defends Their Rights* (New York: Four Winds Press, 1982), p. 104.

Bibliography

Barnouw, Erik. *The Sponsor: Notes on a Modern Potentate.* New York: Oxford University Press, 1978.

Berger, Melvin. *Censorship.* New York: Franklin Watts, Inc., 1982.

Cohn, Nik. *Rock From the Beginning.* New York: Stein and Day, 1969.

Downs, Robert B., ed. *The First Freedom.* Chicago: American Library Association, 1960.

Epstein, Sam, and Beryl Epstein. *Kids in Court: The ACLU Defends Their Rights.* New York: Four Winds Press, 1982.

Evans, J. Edward. *Freedom of Speech.* Minneapolis: Lerner Publications Co., 1990.

———. *Freedom of the Press.* Minneapolis: Lerner Publications Co., 1990.

"Farewell, Trash, Goodbye, Nielsens." *U.S. News and World Report,* (May 15, 1989), pp. 14–15.

Goldman, David J. *The Freedom of the Press in America.* Minneapolis: Lerner Publications Co., 1968.

Hamlin, David. *The Nazi/Skokie Conflict.* Boston: Beacon Press, 1980.

Hentoff, Nat. *The First Freedom: The Tumultuous History of Free Speech in America.* New York: Delacorte Press, 1980.

———. *Free Speech for Me—But Not for Thee.* New York: HarperCollins, Publishers, 1992.

Hohnenberg, John. *Free Press/Free People.* New York: Columbia University Press, 1971.

Hoyt, Olga G., and Edwin P. Hoyt. *Censorship in America.* New York: Seabury Press, 1970.

Jordan, Winthrop, Miriam Greenblatt, and John S. Bowes. *The Americans: The History of a People and a Nation.* Chicago: Science Research Associates, Inc., 1982.

Kilpatrick, James. "Free Speech: Shockjock Pushes Limits on Decency Over the Cliff." *The Milwaukee Journal,* (December 29, 1992), p. A-7.

Latham, Frank B. *The Trial of John Peter Zenger, August, 1735.* New York: Franklin Watts, Inc., 1970.

Leland, John, and Linda Buckley. "Number One With a Bullet." *Newsweek,* (July 1, 1991), p. 63.

Lieberman, Jethro K. *Free Speech, Free Press, and the Law.* New York: Lothrop, Lee & Shepard Books, 1980.

Lindop, Edmund. *The Bill of Rights and Landmark Cases.* New York: Franklin Watts, Inc., 1989.

Locke, Deborah. "Teen Escaped Rumors at School by Taking Life." *Milwaukee Journal,* (November 29, 1992), pp. 1, 30.

Mathews, Tom. "Fine Art or Foul?" *Newsweek,* (July 2, 1990), pp. 46–52.

Minton, Lynn. *Movie Guide for Puzzled Parents.* New York: Delta, 1984.

Moody, Kate. *Growing Up on Television: The TV Effect.* New York: Times Books, 1980.

O'Neil, Robert M. *Classrooms in the Crossfire.* Bloomington: Indiana University Press, 1981.

123

Rogers, Donald J. *Banned! Book Censorship in the Schools.* New York: Julian Messner, 1988.

Salvatore, Nick. *Eugene V. Debs: Citizen and Socialist.* Urbana: University of Illinois Press, 1982.

Schumach, Murray. *The Face on the Cutting Room Floor.* New York: William Morrow & Co., Inc., 1964.

Seligmann, Jean, and Tessa Namuth. "A Limit on the Student Press." *Newsweek,* (January 25, 1988), p. 60.

"The Supreme Court: Bad News for Smut Peddlers." *Time,* (April 1, 1966), p. 57.

"Trigger Happy." *Time,* (January 11, 1993), p. 14.

West's Supreme Court Reporter. St. Paul: West Publishing, 1919–1992.

"Why Johnny Can't Speak." *The Nation,* (January 30, 1988), p. 1.

Zoglin, Richard. "Putting a Brake on TV 'Sleaze.'" *Time,* (March 20, 1989), p. 51.

Further Reading

Epstein, Sam, and Beryl Epstein. *Kids in Court: The ACLU Defends Their Rights.* New York: Four Winds Press, 1982. This book gives a detailed account of how and why the American Civil Liberties Union was founded, then examines constitutional cases in which children were defended by the ACLU. It includes a number of free speech cases.

Evans, J. Edward. *Freedom of the Press.* Minneapolis: Lerner Publications Co., 1990. Evans examines the attempts made to silence the press over the last 200 years.

Kronenwetter, Michael. *Free Press v. Fair Trial.* New York: Franklin Watts, 1986. The struggle between the news media's right to tell a story, the public's right to know, and the right of an accused person to a fair trial is examined in this book. It discusses all forms of media, including television cameras in the courtroom.

Latham, Frank B. *The Trial of John Peter Zenger, August, 1735.* New York: Franklin Watts, Inc., 1970. Latham gives an extensive background on the first newspapers in the colonies, then focuses on Zenger, his arrest, and most important, his trial.

Lieberman, Jethro K. *Free Speech, Free Press, and the Law.* New York: Lothrop, Lee & Shepard Books, 1980. This book includes many free speech cases that are not mentioned in most children's books. It is a particularly good reference for public disturbance and nonverbal speech cases.

Rogers, Donald J. *Banned! Book Censorship in the Schools.* New York: Julian Messner, 1988. Rogers gives many examples of book censorship in the schools, books meant for classroom use as well as library books.

And finally, few days go by without a free speech case being heard somewhere. Check newspapers and current events magazines such as *Time* or *U.S. News and World Report* for up-to-date conflicts over the First Amendment.

Index